CONTENTS

KU-236-825

INTRODUCTION   vi
How to use this Book   vi
Begin reading the author   vi
How to approach unfamiliar or difficult texts   vi
Using biographical material   vi
Vocabulary   vii
Summary   vii

CHAPTER 1: WHY READ JOYCE TODAY?   1
Too obscure for the ordinary reader?   1
Importance and influence   2
Dazzling array of styles   3
Summary   4

CHAPTER 2: BIOGRAPHY   5
Decline in family fortunes   5
Joyce's sexual drive   7
Death of mother   7
Nora Barnacle   8
Life a struggle   8
The writing of *Ulysses*   9
Declining health   9

CHAPTER 3: HOW TO APPROACH JOYCE'S WORK   11
Reading *Dubliners*   11
Reading *Portrait of the Artist*   12
Reading *Ulysses*   12
Summary   13

CHAPTER 4: MAJOR WORKS I: *DUBLINERS*   14
Background to *Dubliners*   14
The theme of paralysis   15

Organisation of *Dubliners* 16

Epiphanies 18

The author's voice 19

Irony 20

'The Dead' 21

Summary 22

CHAPTER 5: MAJOR WORKS II: *A PORTRAIT OF THE ARTIST AS A YOUNG MAN* 23

Background to *Portrait* 23

Autobiography 24

Why Stephen Dedalus? 24

Structure 25

Stephen and his parents 26

Stephen and women 27

Stephen and authority 28

The author's voice 29

Summary 30

CHAPTER 6: MAJOR WORKS III: *ULYSSES* 31

Background to *Ulysses* 31

First reading 32

Structure: the Homeric parallel 33

A comic epic 35

Stephen Dedalus 36

Leopold Bloom 36

Contrasting figures 37

Complementing each other 37

The episodes of *Ulysses* 38

Stream of consciousness 44

Following threads 45

For a first reading 46

Summary 48

Contents

CHAPTER 7: CONTEMPORARY CRITICAL APPROACHES 49
An elaborate joke 50
Initial reactions to *Dubliners* and *Portrait* 50
Initial reactions to *Ulysses* 53
Outrage and insight 54
Gibert reveals the structure 55
Budgen's insights into character 56
Practical and new criticism 57
Poetry as a means of redemption 58
Further critical studies 59
Summary 60

CHAPTER 8: MODERN CRITICAL APPROACHES 61
Theory 61
Joyce and feminist criticism 63
The women in *Dubliners* 65
Joyce and psychoanalytical criticism 69
Analysis of *Portrait* 71
Summary 72

CHAPTER 9: WHERE NEXT? 73
The books 73
Biography 74
Criticism 74
Sources and backgrounds 75
Other media 76
Summary 77

GLOSSARY 78
CHRONOLOGY OF MAJOR WORKS 79
FURTHER READING 80
INDEX 82

Introduction

HOW TO USE THIS BOOK
The *Beginner's Guide* series aims to introduce readers to the major writers of the past 500 years. It is assumed that readers will begin with little or no knowledge and will want to go on to explore the subject in other ways.

BEGIN READING THE AUTHOR
This book is a companion guide to Joyce's major works: it is not a substitute for reading the books themselves. This book is divided into chapters. After considering how to approach the author's work and a brief biography, we go on to explore three of Joyce's main works, *Dubliners*, *Portrait of the Artist as a Young Man* and *Ulysses* before examining some critical approaches to the author. The survey finishes with suggestions for further reading and possible areas of further study.

HOW TO APPROACH UNFAMILIAR OR DIFFICULT TEXTS
Coming across a new writer such as Joyce may seem daunting, but do not be put off. The trick is to persevere. Much good writing is multi-layered and complex. It is precisely this diversity and complexity which makes literature rewarding and exhilarating.

Literature often needs to be read more than once, and in different ways. This is particularly so of Joyce since his style and techniques such as stream of consciousness writing can make it difficult always to be aware of exactly what is going on as you read. Frank Startup provides suggestions as to how best to tackle these difficulties and how to read Joyce for both enjoyment and learning.

USING BIOGRAPHICAL MATERIAL
Opinions differ about whether it is useful to know something of a writer's life and times before reading a text. It can certainly be fascinating to know something about an author. The information gleaned can be illuminating but it can also be irrelevant and misleading and should

be treated with caution. It might be that the author wishes us to engage primarily with the text itself which is usually offered to the public with little meaningful biographical content. It should be possible with most authors to enjoy their work without knowing anything about them. Indeed, one strand of modern literary criticism argues that the author is entirely irrelevant to a text.

VOCABULARY

You will see that **key terms** and unfamiliar words are set in **bold** text. These words are defined and explained in the glossary to be found at the back of the book. In order to help you further we have also included a **summary** of each chapter.

You can read this introductory guide in its entirety, or dip in wherever suits you. You can read it in any order. It is a tool to help you appreciate a key figure in literature. We hope you enjoy reading it and find it useful.

---

* * * *SUMMARY* * * *

To maximise the use of this book:

- Read the author's work.

- Read it several times in different ways.

- Be open to innovative or unusual forms of writing.

- Persevere.

- Treat biographical information with care and deal mainly with the texts themselves.

Rob Abbott and Charlie Bell
Series Editors

Why Read Joyce Today?

Not to have read *Dubliners*, *Portrait of the Artist as a Young Man* and, particularly, *Ulysses*, is to have missed one of the most intellectually absorbing and emotionally rewarding experiences in literature. Joyce was, arguably, the most influential writer of the twentieth century, and writers as diverse as Virginia Woolf, T.S. Eliot, Anthony Burgess and John Updike, among countless others, owe something of their styles, approaches, techniques and even subjects to his pioneering work.

If ever a writer has been misrepresented, it is James Joyce. In his own time, he wrote in poverty and, for the most part, in virtual exile. His work was refused by publishers who feared libel, burned by customs officers, prosecuted for obscenity and consistently misunderstood by people who should have known better. His writing was championed only by the few who understood its importance and the potentially revolutionary effect it would have upon the world of literature – among them W.B. Yeats, Ezra Pound and, in particular, Harriet Shaw Weaver, editor of *The Egoist*.

TOO OBSCURE FOR THE ORDINARY READER?
If Joyce was not read widely before his death because of ignorance, he has not been read after his death because his work has been considered

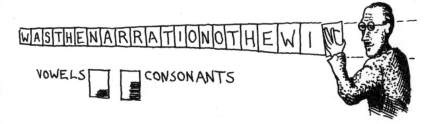

Joyce made large compound words.

too recondite for the ordinary reader, and rather the province of the academic. The importance of Joyce to 'the canon' is now recognised in every university and by every English professor in the world. The richly allusive language of *Ulysses*, its variety of techniques and intricate network of **symbolic** structures have been analysed and dissected in thousands of academic treatises and studies,

> **KEYWORD**
>
> **Symbol** A sign which represents something else. In *Ulysses*, Nelson's Pillar, then standing in Dublin, might be seen as a symbol of colonial triumphalism and oppression.

published or unpublished. The origins of the book, its development, the length of time it was in the writing have all been explored, along with the great pains taken over geographical, historical, mythological, theological and even musical accuracy in the composition of the book. There are differences in interpretations and approaches between authors who write about Joyce, and each new edition claims to be more accurate than the last. What is the general reader, faced with a book which not only looks impenetrable, but has this amount of controversy surrounding it, to do?

Paradoxically, it is the academic attention that Joyce has received and the recognition of his stature as an artist, which, combined with the undeniable difficulties present in approaching *Ulysses*, have tended to repel the intelligent, informed reader who has been led to believe that the book is inaccessible to all those without strings of letters after their names. Even those who have read *Dubliners* with pleasure, or at least appreciation, and have studied *Portrait of the Artist as a Young Man* at A-level, throw up their hands at a contemplation of *Ulysses*, thinking it either the province of academics only, or staggering through the first quarter of the books only to exclaim 'Life's too short' and reach for the nearest thriller instead. This is a shame and a great mistake.

IMPORTANCE AND INFLUENCE

Let us begin with the recognition of Joyce's importance and his influence on all that followed him. Let us recognise that, among other achievements, he is a bridge between the realistic English novels of the nineteenth century and the experimental European writers. He broke down barriers between autobiography and fiction, putting himself, his experiences and his environment into his writing as no one, as far as we know, had done before.

Dubliners is a collection of 15 short stories set in Dublin in the early years of the twentieth century. The subject matter is the city and its inhabitants, and the stories are portraits, miniatures, linked by themes and characters which recur throughout Joyce's writing. *Portrait of the Artist as a Young Man* concentrates on the character of Stephen Dedalus, and the experiences which formed him: a picture of how cultural, religious, political and environmental influences combine with personal experience to shape an individual. These two books are synthesised in *Ulysses*, a work of thematic and symbolic density, but also of great humanity and humour.

DAZZLING ARRAY OF STYLES
Ulysses presents the most complete portrait of a fictional character in literature, exploring his past and present, his conscious experiences, memories, desires, fears, aspirations, dreams – conscious and unconscious – as he lives one day of his life in Dublin in 1904. The psychological realism is placed in a universal context through the exploration of many important themes, such as fatherhood, betrayal and loyalty, and in a particular context through a wonderful portrayal of a particular city, Dublin, and its citizens. All this is explored in a dazzling array of styles and registers. And the whole is rich, complete, not to be put off until later, but to be read now and savoured later, again and again. Joyce should be regarded not only as a technician of immense versatility and power. He is also a novelist whose characters and situations affect, move and absorb the reader as do those of more conventional and accessible authors, only at a deeper level, being more complex and profound.

In *Ulysses*, Myles Crawford, newspaper editor, is discussing literature with Stephen Dedalus, writer searching for the inspiration and impetus to write. He says: 'Give them something with a bite in it. Put us all into it, damn its soul, Father, Son and Holy Ghost and Jakes McCarthy.' This is exactly what Joyce did: in all three books, and, later, in the enigmatic *Finnegans Wake*. The place, the time, the people, the history, the politics, the religion, the macrocosm, the microcosm, you, me and, of course, Jakes McCarthy. First, he was reviled for it, and then lionised for it. He has not, however, been thought of, as Shakespeare and Dickens are, as part of a heritage in which the general reader can share.

❉ ❉ ❉ ❉*SUMMARY* ❉ ❉ ❉ ❉

- Joyce is one of the most influential authors of the twentieth century.

- He employed and instigated techniques which have influenced the whole course of modern fiction.

- He wanted his books to be read by everyone.

- He broke down barriers between autobiography and fiction.

- He presented the most complete portrait of a fictional character ever.

- His psychological realism is extraordinary.

- His technical innovations are immense.

- You will enjoy him.

Biography

2

In his poem 'Who's Who', W.H. Auden wrote, 'A shilling life will give you all the facts', but, as the poem says, mere facts can only beg larger questions and point to greater mysteries. How can 'a shilling life' convey anything of the complexity and power of what Richard Ellman (1959) called one of the most 'rarefied' minds of the century? To understand Shakespeare, we have very little except the works: with James Joyce, we are luckier. We have excellent biographies, memoirs and critiques written by people who knew him, including Stanislaus, his brother, and we have his letters.

Joyce was born in 1882, the second child of John Stanislaus Joyce and May Joyce, nee Murray: the first child, John, had died at birth, as would seven others of the 17 children born to the Joyces. The family enjoyed a comfortable middle-class life, living in the south Dublin suburbs and, for a while, in the seaside town of Bray. Joyce had a governess and, at the age of six, entered the famous Conglowes Wood College, a renowned Jesuit school.

He was a happy, outgoing child with a doting and somewhat anxious mother. At Conglowes he appeared devout and hard working. Having to fend for himself in a school full of boys run under a strict regime, he learnt some hard lessons which clearly stayed with him and which he explored thoroughly in *Portrait of the Artist.*

DECLINE IN FAMILY FORTUNES

These lessons were soon to be underlined by events at home. John Joyce's family had lived comfortably because, as well as having some private means, he received a good salary from a local government post which he had held since 1880. In 1891 this salary was terminated, and the family fortunes went into permanent decline. James Joyce was, in his third year, removed from Conglowes and the family moved back to Dublin from Bray. James was enrolled in the Christian Brothers School.

Still devout and diligent, Joyce supplemented his school work by read-ing widely, learning summaries of historical events, studying lists of Latin or French words and writing. He showed most promise at com-position, and won several prizes, allowing him to make contributions to the family funds, buying necessities or providing occasional treats.

This decline in fortune and his parents' reaction to it were to affect Joyce deeply. Scholastically he was as diligent as ever, and his obvious-ly superior intellect and ability led to his being given a free place at Belvedere College in Dublin. At first, all was well: he was noted for his academic excellence and his piety, but this was to change rapidly.

Throughout this period, the growing family moved frequently, each new location being slightly less salubrious than the last. John Joyce's reaction to all this was fierce defiance: he considered his fallen position a betrayal, and identified himself with the disgraced nationalist hero, **Parnell**. In *Portrait*, there is a vivid account of a political argument over the Christmas dinner table about the betrayal of Parnell in which the voice of John Joyce can clearly be heard. John Joyce would not live within his means, he was frustrated and angry and life became a round of desperate attempts to borrow money, tap influence and present a bold, brave front. He drank, he blustered, he grew violent – on one ter-rible occasion, after the death of the son Frederick, he tried to strangle his wife and had to be restrained by James. She, however, bore all this trouble with the patience of the devout believer in God's will.

KEY FACT

Parnell, Charles Stewart (1846–91). Leading figure in the Irish Parliamentary party who united most of the Irish Nationalist groups and made the British Parliament consider Home Rule for Ireland. He was disgraced following his citation in the divorce case of one of his associates, Captain O'Shea and his wife, Kitty, whom he subsequently married. Parnell's fall and the immediate collapse of nationalist aspirations rings throughout Joyce's work.

JOYCE'S SEXUAL DRIVE

In the midst of all this upheaval, uncertainty and violence, James Joyce was also wrestling with a powerful sexual drive. His sexual awareness had been aroused when he was 12, and there had been an incident following which his mother had discharged a maid in the family's employ. Then, in 1896, at the age of 14, he first visited a prostitute, and the battle between release and guilt began. Although he spent time in retreat and in confession following his sexual encounter, belief slipped away and he broke with the Church. This took him further from his mother, and he became impatient with her saintly forbearance, preferring the bluster and defiance of his father who was, at least, still fighting, shouting and singing. He came to identify more with his father as they were both sinners, while he identified his mother with the repressive Church and its system which had turned her into a victim.

DEATH OF MOTHER

By this time Joyce had become a student at University College, Dublin, studying English, Italian and French, and although he was only 20, had read almost everything. He discovered Ibsen and admired him. He wrote an article on Ibsen for the *Fortnightly Review* for which he received 12 guineas, and was greatly encouraged by a favourable response from Ibsen himself. He wrote poems and attempted to make contact with the great Irish literary figures of the day, but, after graduating and receiving his BA in 1902, he decided to study medicine and left for Paris intending to support himself by teaching English. In April 1903, he was called home by a brief telegram. His mother's cancer was approaching its final stages and she was dying. Joyce borrowed the money for his fare and returned to Dublin. On his arrival, his mother pleaded with him to take confession and receive communion: he refused. She died that August.

During the next year or so, Joyce stayed in Dublin. He continued to write, reviewing books and began *Stephen Hero*, the autobiographical novel which was to become *Portrait of the Artist as a Young Man*. Joyce continued to roister around Dublin with his friends, including Oliver Gogarty, with whom he lodged for a while in a Martello Tower, and who was to be represented in *Ulysses* as Buck Mulligan. In 1904, his life was to change utterly and permanently when he met Nora Barnacle, the woman with whom he would spend the rest of his life.

NORA BARNACLE

Nora Barnacle was 20 years old when she met Joyce. She had been born and raised in Galway, was virtually unschooled and was working in Dublin as a chambermaid in Finn's Hotel after having run away from home. Nora did not appear at the first arranged meeting, leaving Joyce waiting for her, but they did meet on 16 June 1904, when they walked, talked and, as Joyce later told her 'You made me a man' (letter to Nora Joyce, 7 August 1909 in *Selected Letters*, ed. Ellman, p. 159). This day was to be immortalised in Ulysses as the day on which Mr Bloom met Stephen Dedalus in Dublin – 'Bloomsday'.

Knowing that the relationship would never be tolerated in Dublin, and failing to raise money from Dublin's literary circle, he and Nora left to live on the continent. His father did not find out about the relationship until after they had sailed and his reaction was just as Joyce had expected. Ireland had failed to recognise and support his genius, and he left it, but the disappointment and anger he felt would show itself in his work.

LIFE A STRUGGLE

From this point, the Joyces moved between Zurich and Trieste, with Joyce earning money by writing and teaching, as well as raising money by borrowing. Letters home to his younger brother, Stanislaus, show that life was a struggle. In 1905 a son, Giorgio, was born, and, a year later, *Dubliners* was finished and the revision of *Stephen Hero* as *Portrait* had begun. Stanislaus joined the family in Trieste and, despite James Joyce's tendency to drink whatever was earned, the pooling of financial resources eased the situation slightly. In 1907 Nora gave birth to a daughter, Lucia.

Between 1909 and 1914, Joyce and his family returned to Dublin at various times to visit relatives, try to raise money, inaugurate business ventures which were heroically unsuccessful and see his work published. *Dubliners* made people nervous, however: its representation of the city and its citizens was not flattering, and some of its subject matter was considered improper. Cuts were demanded, law suits were feared and the collection of stories did not appear until 1914, at the same time as *Portrait* began serialisation in *The Egoist*. Joyce had found a champion and patron in the editor, Harriet Shaw Weaver. Her generosity to him was to continue for the rest of his life. In 1915 the Joyces left Ireland for Zurich, never to return.

THE WRITING OF ULYSSES

Joyce's masterpiece, *Ulysses*, was begun in 1914 and serialisation of it in the *Little Review* magazine began in 1918, with the help of Ezra Pound and Harriet Shaw Weaver. Once again, however, enterprise was thwarted when, in 1921, a court case brought serialisation to a halt on the grounds of obscenity. It was to be published first in its complete version in 1922 in Paris, where the Joyces were living, by Sylvia Beach's bookshop 'Shakespeare and Company'. It was not published in America until 1934 and not in Britain until 1936.

DECLINING HEALTH

Joyce's eyesight was poor.

Throughout this time, Joyce's health was failing. Attacks of glaucoma were destroying his eyesight, despite operations to rescue it. He suffered from arthritis and had all his teeth removed and replaced with permanent plates, but, nevertheless, work commenced on *Finnegans Wake* and *Pomes Penyeach* was published in 1927.

In 1931 Joyce and Nora married in Paris, but over the Christmas period of that year John Joyce died, aged 80, throwing Joyce, who had refused to send his father money after the publication of *Ulysses*, into a confusion of grief and guilt. More sadness came in 1932 when Lucia was diagnosed as schizophrenic. Much care and attention was lavished on cures for her, including sessions with Jung, but her condition never improved, and she died in a Northampton hospital in 1982. *Finnegans Wake* was published in London and New York in 1939 and was received with indifference or incomprehension.

On 7 January 1941, Joyce was taken ill with stomach cramps and at 2.15 on 13 January 1941 he died of complications following an operation for a perforated duodenal ulcer.

Joyce never fully recognised his daughter's madness.

How to Approach Joyce's Work

IN A WORD – CAREFULLY!

On a first reading of many books, the reader is often tempted to skim in order to get the main ideas of the narrative – or simply to find out what happens next. Joyce does not reward skim reading: he deals in nuance of atmosphere and character created by a careful and deliberate choice of words, rather than linear plots. Any reader who attempts to skim is likely to reach the end of a story in *Dubliners*, a section of *Portrait* or even a paragraph of *Ulysses* and wonder what on earth he or she has just read.

Each of these books is a work of art in its own right and can, of course, be read independently and separately from the others, but it is most rewarding to treat them as an organic whole to see how breathtaking and original is the vision. Over the years, the remarkable unity of Joyce's work has been established, and, if you intend to read all three of the books which are treated here, it is best to read them in order, treating each one as a continuation and expansion of the previous. Characters and scenes appearing in *Dubliners* will reappear in *Ulysses*. The atmospheres created in *Dubliners* will pervade passages of both *Portrait* and *Ulysses*. The story of the main character of *Portrait* is continued in *Ulysses* against a background established in *Dubliners*.

READING DUBLINERS

Dubliners is maybe best seen as an exploration of place. Dublin in the early twentieth century, its inhabitants, its geography, its politics and religion, its streets and houses, its pubs and restaurants, is more than just a backdrop against which a series of events is played, or characters move. Dublin, and Joyce's view of it, is part of the action, part of the character of all three books. As you read *Dubliners*, it might help to keep a note of locations, areas, different parts of the city. Joyce is meticulous about location and frequently describes routes taken through the city: indeed, *Ulysses* is one long route through the city, an odyssey through Dublin. Joyce said that it would be possible for future readers to reconstruct a map of the Dublin of 1904 from no source other than his books. A first reading should, therefore, be closely aware of setting and should treat characters in *Dubliners* as part of the fabric of the city: many of them will recur in *Ulysses*, and pleasure in that book will be heightened as the reader meets such people as Lenehan and Corley again, or hears more of Bob Doran and Julia Morkan.

READING PORTRAIT OF THE ARTIST

If *Dubliners* is best seen at this stage as an exploration of setting, *Portrait* is an exploration of character and the way in which different influences shape and develop the artist in question – Stephen Dedalus. The reader will come to know Stephen well, but observe him in the third person rather than have access to his own interpretation of events in the first person. This distance encourages objectivity and the reader will be able to make judgements about Stephen and his behaviour which he would not be able to make about himself. Careful reading of *Portrait* will make the notoriously difficult opening episodes of *Ulysses* much more accessible, particularly if key scenes and names are remembered.

READING ULYSSES

Ulysses poses its own problems: a careful reading of the first two books will lessen confusion, but still, the stream of consciousness techniques used by Joyce will lead to difficulties. Much of the book is spent in the minds of Stephen, Leopold Bloom or his wife, Molly, recording apparently random thoughts, memories, impressions and passing emotions. These may well be triggered by sights and sounds which make plain to the reader how the trains of thought have begun and how they might develop, but they frequently lead to memories whose significance may not become apparent until later in the book, or which may refer back to some apparently obscure thought earlier in the book – or even in previous books.

This will be dealt with more closely in the chapter on *Ulysses*, but, for the time being, the advice remains: read carefully; store information; be prepared to go back and re-read; forget the notion of plot as a linear progression through a sequence of events; be alert to nuance and **allusion**; note recurring images and see how symbolic significance is built.

KEYWORD

Allusion Indirect reference. Joyce's books are full of echoes of his own life, other works of literature, myths, biblical stories and so on. Much research has been done on allusions in Joyce.

❋ ❋ ❋ ❋ *SUMMARY* ❋ ❋ ❋ ❋

- Don't be put off by apparent difficulties.

- Read carefully.

- Keep note of characters and places.

- Be prepared to reread both sections and chapters.

- Keep note of recurring images or themes.

4 Major Works 1: Dubliners

BACKGROUND TO DUBLINERS

Dubliners is a collection of 15 stories written between 1904 and 1907. Three of them were published in *The Irish Homestead* in 1904, but the rest, and all 15 as a collection, did not appear until 1914. They were accepted for publication in 1906 by Grant Richards but there followed an eight-year struggle with printers and publishers who objected to some of the language and the images, and who feared charges of blasphemy and libel. Amendments were asked for, refused, argued over, conceded until, amazingly, in 1912, the printer destroyed the 1000 copies he had produced rather than be associated with the book. By this time, Richards was ready to publish and an edition taken from a partially corrected copy of proof sheets for the final version was prepared. One copy of the destroyed 1912 edition survives and the corrections incorporated in it

Joyce looked at lifes' underbelly in *Dubliners*.

were published in the 1967 edition by Jonathan Cape, which also retained the punctuation Joyce preferred, most notably the use of dashes to replace the inverted commas which introduce dialogue and which Joyce referred to as 'perverted commas'.

Leaving aside wrangles over the use of the word 'bloody' and objections to such images as 'she changed the position of her legs often', which exasperated Joyce and arose from contemporary notions of decency which seem rather quaint now, it is not difficult to see why people were nervous about *Dubliners*. The book's deliberate geographical accuracy is such that establishments and even individuals might be easily identifiable from the text and the portrayal of the city and its inhabitants is far from flattering.

THE THEME OF PARALYSIS

Joyce wanted to portray what he saw as the paralysis of the city and of life in it. Joyce's Dublin is a backwater, a place in which people are trapped, their ambitions frustrated and their futures confined. His term for this condition was **hemiplegia**, and it is shown in the stories in a variety of ways.

KEYWORD

Hemiplegia a medical term employed by Joyce to represent what he saw as the paralysis affecting Dublin and its citizens.

The most obvious and literal example is in the story 'Eveline'. As the story opens, Eveline is sitting at her window reflecting upon her life as she contemplates leaving home. She is leaving to marry 'manly, open-hearted Frank' and live with him in Buenos Aires. As we follow her thoughts, it becomes clear that her life is miserable: her work at the stores is menial and her supervisor is unkind to her, 'especially whenever there were people listening', her mother is dead and she has the responsibility of looking after two young children. She also has to take care of her father, who is selfish, sometimes drunk and violent.

Eveline sees marriage as something that will bring the respect that she lacks – self-respect as well as respect from others – but the cycle of dependency, responsibility and the denial of the spirit is shown time and again in marriage, whether through the control which dominating mothers exercise over their children in 'The Boarding House' and 'A Mother', or in the sort of vicious circle presented in 'Counterparts' in which Farrington, humiliated by and angry with his own life and circumstances, returns home to vent his frustration physically upon his family. Where Eveline, at 19, justifies her inability to escape her situation by thinking of happier times and with the possibility that things might improve, Farrington has no hope left. The only escapes left to him are drink and violence. Both Farrington and Eveline in their own ways are caught in the stasis of Dublin. This they have in common with all other characters in the book: the stultification caused by the constraints placed upon the individual spirit due to religious teaching and social expectation in Dublin, 'such a small city: everyone knows everyone else's business'.

Joyce made his intentions clear in his correspondence with Grant Richards in which he accused the reluctant publisher of 'preventing the Irish people from having one good look at themselves in my nicely polished looking glass' (letter to Grant Richards, 23 June 1906 in *Selected Letters*, op cit p. 90).

ORGANISATION OF DUBLINERS

Progression from childhood

In the same correspondence Joyce describes *Dubliners* as a moral history and saw it as the first step towards the spiritual liberation of his country. The implication is that before liberation is possible, the nature and the effects of the trap must be understood. While the theme of a city and its people in stasis unifies the stories, the cohesion is created by the organisation of the stories within the collection.

There is a progression through the stories from childhood to maturity, from the early experiences of characters whose lives are before them, to the despair or resignation of middle-aged characters caught in the atmosphere of the city.

The cycle of disillusionment

As you read the first three stories, you might like to think about how they show the beginnings of the cycle of disillusionment which becomes established in later stories. In each, potentially positive experiences are tarnished. Although the boy in 'The Sisters' is confused about his relationship with the dying priest, he appreciates that the priest has 'taught him a great deal'. By the time we have reached the end of the story and he has listened, half-understanding, to the conversations of his sceptical uncle and friend, and to the account of the priest's sisters, it is the less positive impressions of the priest which have been reinforced. Similarly, in 'An Encounter', the excitement and sense of adventure at the beginning of the story is lost when the incomprehensible adult world, in the shape of a pervert, whose fantasies about chastisement bewilder and embarrass the boy, leave him with an undefined sense of corruption.

'Araby' begins with the romantic dreams of a boy infatuated by his friend's sister. These feelings become concentrated upon the exotic-sounding Araby bazaar and the boy's promise to bring something back from it to the object of his adoration. Again, as in the previous stories, the promise of something exciting or with fulfilling potential is dissipated in a tawdry and dispiriting actuality. In this case, disillusionment transfers itself to his initial feelings and the story finishes with his seeing himself 'as a creature driven and derided by vanity; and my eyes burned with anger and anguish'. He sees his adoration of the young girl as folly and equates it with his previous view of the bazaar as something exotic and splendid: the vividness of the internal vision has, again, been let down by reality, a theme which will recur in *Portrait*.

From young adults to maturity

From these initial stories of childhood experience, we move to four stories, beginning with 'Eveline', about young adults and then to four stories which concern mature people. The next three show us characters involved in public life or public situations and for the final story, 'The Dead', we move into the world of Dublin's cultured urbanites, finding yet more paralysis of will and action, although with hints of escape.

In addition to following this overall progression, it is interesting to look across the stories to see, for example, the variety of ways in which Joyce provides his characters with reminders of other worlds, from the fragmentary dream of 'some land where customs were strange' in 'The Sisters' to the fake exotica of the bazaar in 'Araby' and the London woman in 'Counterparts': from elopement with Frank in 'Eveline' to the apparently cosmopolitan and sophisticated Gallagher in 'A Little Cloud' and the driving team in 'After the Race'. In each case, however, in some way or another, the characters are reminded of their own provincialism and inadequacies.

It is also interesting to see how we are able to contrast different characters in similar situations, for example, how Little Chandler in 'A Little Cloud' and Farrington in 'Counterparts' behave with their families, or to compare the relationships between mothers and daughters in 'A Mother' and 'The Boarding House'.

EPIPHANIES

Epiphany comes from the Greek word meaning 'manifestation' and, in the Church, refers to the revelation of Christ's divinity to the Magi. Joyce uses the word to mean the sudden revelation of truth or self-awareness in a moment, an action, a word, a thought, in itself possibly trivial, but loaded with significance for the

> **KEYWORD**
>
> Epiphany The word Joyce uses to describe a moment in which an experience reveals its inner meaning.

receiver, if the receiver is alive to it and its importance. Some epiphanies are unavoidable: at the end of the card game in 'After the Race', Jimmy Doyle, his head resting in his hands, 'glad of the dark stupor that would cover up his folly', is awoken by the cry 'Daybreak, gentlemen', and the realisation of what he has done – and, possibly, that he has been cheated. Sometimes the epiphany is one of awakening to disillusionment, as the boy sees himself at the end of 'Araby', but it may also carry the hint of redemption through the acceptance of a sometimes painful truth.

The epiphany of Mr Duffy

In 'A Painful Case', Mr Duffy is a man who has his life under control. He hates 'anything which betokened physical or mental disorder'. He has 'neither companions, nor friends, church nor creed'. He is a model of self-containment. Mr Duffy's image of himself is conveyed to us in detail, and may, at first glance, appear to be different from other Dubliners: he is in control of his life, content and self-sufficient. Between the lines, however, Joyce allows us to see him for the self-deceiving prig that he is. His encounter with someone whose misery is genuine, and to whose need he fails to respond, provides an epiphany which leaves him aware of his own loneliness: 'He felt his moral nature falling to pieces.'

At other times, potential epiphanies are ignored or denied: Eveline has closed herself off from any realisation of her situation, while the craven Lenehan, in 'Two Gallants', sees the desperation of his position as he feels 'tired of knocking about, of pulling the devil by the tail, of shifts and intrigues'. This moment of self-knowledge is soon lost, however, as he dreams not just of living happily with a 'good simple-minded girl', but of one with 'a little of the ready'.

THE AUTHOR'S VOICE

Joyce does not moralise or tell us what to think. The purpose of literature, for him, is to reveal: the author presents truthfully, and the reader observes, infers and draws conclusions. His books are neither philosophical treatises nor statements of ethical positions. Joyce is not a Fielding, halting the narrative to reflect upon the behaviour of the characters, neither is he a Jane Austen, making direct observations upon the society about which he is writing. There is no consistent authorial voice in *Dubliners*. Each story is told from a different perspective and we view events from different points of view.

The first three stories, for example, are told in the first person, so that we only see or hear what the main character sees or hears. We do not see what the 'queer old josser' in 'An Encounter' is doing, because the narrator does not look up. We are, however, given the ability to *understand* more than the narrator does: in 'The Sisters', although we may only be able to hear what the boy hears, we are able to interpret it in ways impossible for the boy, and also to understand the effect it is having on the boy. In 'A Painful Case', we are let in to Mr. Duffy's thoughts and form an impression of him. Although we are told, from his perspective, of the behaviour of Mrs Sinico, we are able to interpret it and understand it in a way that Mr Duffy cannot.

IRONY

This obliqueness, this gap between what the characters believe and the reader understands often leads to **irony**. As we listen to the self-important and cynical talk in 'Ivy Day in the Committee Rooms', we become aware of its emptiness – and when, at the end, Joe Hynes is persuaded to read his eulogy on Parnell in cel-

> **KEYWORD**
>
> Irony A figure of speech in which the implied meaning is the opposite of what has actually been said or written.

ebration of the glorious past, our impressions are confirmed when the poem is revealed to be clichéd doggerel. The story finishes with the dry observation: 'Mr. Crofton said that it was a very fine piece of writing.'

At the same time, we must be alive to the messages which are sent through the careful choice of words to describe settings or the physical appearance of characters. The opening pages of 'Two Gallants' will convey a clear impression of Lenehan and his relationship to Corley without any intervening comment from the author: the image carries the meaning. Similarly, a repetition of images of anger and frustration in 'Counterparts' clearly shows us the state of Farrington's mind. In 'After the Races', we meet Jimmy Doyle, an apparently successful young man who has made money and who moves in cosmopolitan circles. Clues to his character are established in Joyce's description of his past: we learn that his father 'sent' him to school in England; 'sent' him to Dublin University to study law and 'sent' him to Cambridge for a term. His dependency is thus revealed and the ending of the story, which sees him at the mercy of others, does not surprise us.

'THE DEAD'

If the collection begins with stories in which potential good is thwarted and moves on with stories in which efforts to escape – actual and symbolic – are frustrated, it finishes with a story which offers some hope. We are at a Christmas party given by the aunts of Gabriel Conroy. As a change from the previous stories, the atmosphere is cheerful and hospitable, old friends and family are meeting again, a sense of affection is felt. Gabriel is a successful language teacher, a sensitive and considerate man whose observations are always generous and good-natured. During the story, however, he finds his view of himself and his life questioned in various ways. Returning to the hotel at which he is lodging, his wife tells him of her first love – a young man who died for love of her. Gabriel, having been unsettled by the events of the evening and the thoughts they have brought to him, is left to reflect upon his life and his situation. This leads to Gabriel's moment of epiphany – as 'generous tears' fill his eyes, he recognises the comparative blandness of his own world and feelings when compared to those of the dead lover. He sees Dublin as a negation of real life and passion and he decides 'the time had come for him to set out on his journey westward'. Many have equated Gabriel's realisation of his own complacency with Joyce's recognition of his own intensity and noted the subsequent irony and sense of humour which informs the presentation of Stephen in *Portrait*. Others see Gabriel's look westwards as a symbolic reference to the need to find a home in Irish art, rather than in the pseudo-British cultural community in Dublin. Feminist critics have very interesting views about Gabriel's epiphany, but we will return to those later. Most agree, however, that the story ends on a more optimistic note than the others, seeming to suggest the possibility for escape, for change.

In these short stories, we are given a picture of the inertia of life in a city caught in paralysis, every attempt to break out thwarted, every hint of something better frustrated rather than fulfilling. Love, spirituality, intellect, refracted and turned to something meaner, corrupted, constraining rather than liberating. It is in this city that Leopold Bloom and Stephen Dedalus will meet in *Ulysses* for the greatest epiphany of all.

✳ ✳ ✳ ✳ SUMMARY ✳ ✳ ✳ ✳

- *Dubliners* is a collection of 15 stories set in Dublin.

- It portrays the city as a place in which people are trapped.

- Each story shows people in situations which, whether they know it or not, are spiritually and emotionally deadening.

- The stories are an organic whole best read in the order presented.

- The stories progress from childhood through to maturity.

- There are many correspondences and parallels between the stories which are worth tracing.

- Joyce does not moralise about his characters; he presents them to us and we form our own opinions.

- 'The Dead' offers an optimistic conclusion to the stories.

Major Works II: A Portrait of The Artist As A Young Man

BACKGROUND TO PORTRAIT

In 1904, as he was beginning to earn some money from writing, and in the year when three of the short stories which were to form part of *Dubliners* were published, Joyce began work on an autobiographical novel called *Stephen Hero*. This would be abandoned in 1906 and re-worked into what is now *A Portrait of the Artist as a Young Man*. The incomplete original is available and it is interesting to compare it to what it became. *Stephen Hero* is a far more conventional piece of work. It covers the period of Stephen's life as a student and is much longer than the equivalent section in the later version. It is much more explicit, less oblique in its viewpoint than *Portrait*, its descriptions of characters and incidents are more detailed. *Portrait* is a reduction, not just in length, but also in terms of the distillation of experience. *Portrait* first appeared as a serial in *The Egoist* in 1914.

Portrait of the Artist as a Young Man.

AUTOBIOGRAPHY

Joyce's brother, Stanislaus, describes the book as an artistic creation rather than an autobiography. Although events and characters are drawn directly from Joyce's life in detail, we must guard against too close an identification between Joyce and his alter ego, Stephen Dedalus. By all accounts, for example, Joyce himself was a happy, playful child known to his family as 'Sunny Jim': it is difficult to imagine his counterpart being referred to as 'Sunny Stephen'! Until the end of the book, when it seems as if Stephen is beginning to take himself a little less seriously, the character appears to lack Joyce's sense of humour and his ability to see himself objectively. In many ways, this is the point: the novel is an account of the formation and development of an artistic temperament and an artistic theory, and this involves growing into the sort of self-awareness which Stephen begins to achieve by the end. The conventional autobiography, written in the first person and containing nothing but accounts through the eyes and in the words of the writer, leaves little room for any interpretations other than those of the writer. *Portrait*, however, is written in the third person. It shows formative experiences – home, school, college – and formative influences – national history, religion, received moral and ethical codes – as Stephen perceives them, but also gives the reader room to manoeuvre. As we saw in *Dubliners*, in such stories as 'A Painful Case' and 'Clay', it is possible to allow us into the minds of the characters while giving us the ability to stand back and see them as they cannot see themselves. In order fully to appreciate the development of the artist, we must see him developing, whether he is aware of it or not. When, at the end of *Portrait*, Stephen begins to mock slightly his own intensity, he is catching up with the rest of us who had, thanks to Joyce's methods of description and oblique comment, been aware of it all along.

WHY STEPHEN DEDALUS?

The pseudonym Stephen Daedalus, later anglicised to Dedalus, was adopted by Joyce at an early stage. The three *Dubliners* stories published in *The Irish Homestead* in 1904 were submitted under that name.

'Stephen' is the name of the first Christian martyr, stoned to death because he insisted that Christ's authority was greater than that of the Temple, and would concede nothing even under trial and duress. Daedalus, in Greek legend, was an artificer, a smith whose creations included the Labyrinth made to house the Minotaur in Crete. When Daedalus and his son Icarus were imprisoned in Crete, Daedalus fashioned wings with which they could fly away. Icarus, however, flew too close to the Sun, which melted the wax holding the smaller wings together. Icarus fell to his death. The combination of these names, that of a Christian martyr persecuted for his insight by a reactionary institution, and that of a pagan figure who created labyrinthine artifices and then flew away from those who did not understand him, gave Joyce a name redolent with appropriate symbolism.

STRUCTURE

The book has five chapters which are numbered, and each chapter contains a number of sections indicated by an asterisk which separates them. These sections move the reader chronologically through the events and experiences of Stephen's life rather in the manner of a photograph album giving snapshots of significant moments. Each section shows us an experience which contributes to the development of the artist, and each chapter ends with a turning point which is to be instrumental in forming him.

As the boy grows, the language becomes more sophisticated, from the baby talk of the opening lines of Chapter 1 to the exposition of a theory of aesthetics in Chapter 5. We see Stephen as a child, observing what is going on around him, astonished, confused and frightened by the passion and anger shown in a political argument at a family Christmas; becoming acclimatised to life at school, experiencing and dealing with injustice. We experience his growing sexual awareness and the confusion between lust for and idealisation of women, the temporary – and frequent – respite he finds with prostitutes leading him, via a shattering experience at a religious retreat, to repentance and a devoutly religious life. Once the idea of a vocation within the priesthood is raised, however, we follow the thoughts, reflections and insights which formulate the decisions with which the book ends.

STEPHEN AND HIS PARENTS

The first section of the first chapter sketches the family in a series of sense impressions. As Stephen leaves home for Conglowes, the memories are conventional – advice, pocket money and tears – and he is confused by schoolboy questions such as 'What is your father?', which will rebound later, when fortunes decline.

The family

The first sustained image we have of the family occurs in Chapter 1 when Stephen has returned home for Christmas and he, his mother and Dante, the nanny, are waiting for the men to return from their walk to begin Christmas dinner. Joyce begins the section with images of warmth and cheer and shows Stephen listening to mysterious adult talk in a secure family atmosphere. By the end of the meal, however, Stephen, 'raising his terror stricken face, saw that his father's eyes were full of tears'. What has happened is a ferocious argument about the relationship of the Church to national politics which has, inevitably, focused on the fate of Parnell, and which has pitched Dante and the family guest, Mr Casey, at each other in the most immoderate of language, culminating in Dante's statement, 'We won! We crushed him to death! Fiend' and Mr Casey's sobbing cry, 'Poor Parnell! My poor dead king!' Not only is Stephen first struck by the way in which the wider world can impinge on the personal, and by the way in which passions and anger are aroused, but the view which he will later take of his parents begins here.

His parents as individuals

This first view of his parents as individuals grows steadily, heightened by their reactions to the drop in fortunes. In Chapter 2, when Stephen accompanies his father to Cork, he is ashamed of what he sees as his father's sentimentality, his garrulity and his gullibility. As Mr Dedalus banters in clichés with his friends in the pub, flirts with the barmaids and boasts about his son's accomplishments, Stephen sits in an agony of embarrassment. What had been seen as qualities of bonhomie, humour and wit are now seen as shallow and rather pathetic.

Much later, in Chapter 5, when Stephen is at university, we see the family at a low ebb, at breakfast in the kitchen of their latest home, having been reduced to pawning clothes. Stephen seems completely disaffected and his parents locked into their roles, the mother patiently deprecating: 'The dear knows you might try to be on time for your lectures', the father blustering, 'Is your lazy bitch of a brother gone out yet?' In Chapter 5, we learn that, despite his mother's tearful pleas, Stephen has refused to attend Easter communion.

STEPHEN AND WOMEN

Stephen's attitude towards women during the book is contradictory. In the early encounters, there is a mixture of romantic idealism and ill-defined eroticism overlaid with religious imagery. His memories of his childhood friend Eileen in Chapter 1 mix with the notion of the Virgin Mary as a Tower of Ivory with the long, white, slim fingers which Eileen put over his eyes and in his pocket, and the stream of her golden hair as she ran away. He is mysteriously disturbed by Mercedes, the heroine of 'The Count of Monte Cristo', and has romantic fantasies about her in Chapter 2.

In Chapter 2, Stephen meets Emma Clery at a party, but fails, as he sees it, to take the opportunity she offers of kissing her. Instead, he goes home to write a poem about the experience. Emma remains in his thoughts, and we see Stephen two years later, bitterly disappointed that she is not in the audience to watch him perform in his school play. Further sporadic encounters with Emma occur throughout the book in which Stephen imagines himself as being slighted, although in Chapter 5, when Stephen is preparing to leave for Paris, Emma is asking him why they had lost contact.

There is a powerful lust running in Stephen of which he is ashamed and afraid, thinking of it as 'a brutal and individual malady' which conjured up 'monstrous reveries' which sicken and appal him. His first encounter with a prostitute occurs in Chapter 2 when Stephen finds temporary release, both physical and mental.

STEPHEN AND AUTHORITY

Gradually, throughout the book, Stephen's experiences and his view of himself make him distance himself from the world around him, and become more self-absorbed. As his view of his parents is altered so is his view of other areas of authority, such as the Church.

He runs foul of authority in the first chapter, when he is unjustly punished by the overzealous Father Dolan, but secures a victory when he refuses to accept the wrong and, by protesting to the rector, secures the promise that the rector would 'speak to Father Dolan'. His persistence is thus rewarded and he becomes something of a hero with the boys, who cheer him. This is put into perspective later when his father reveals how, in fact, the two priests had enjoyed a 'famous laugh' at the expense of the 'manly little chap'.

Although Stephen knows that his encounters with prostitutes constitute mortal sins, he is able to rationalise it until the three-day school retreat in Chapter 3. The sermons preached by Father Arnall on death, judgement and hell terrify Stephen. Walking the streets in confusion, he takes confession at an anonymous chapel and experiences spiritual release and happiness which, in Chapter 4, lead him to reorganise his life upon lines of devout self-discipline. In this, however, he retains his individuality; his regime is of his own devising because his sin had been from his own defiance.

Time and again in the book, as Stephen grows more apart, we see him deliberately taking up unorthodox positions and opinions, from his controversial championing of Byron in Chapter 2, to his treatment of Davin and McCann in Chapter 5, in response to their political and religious convictions, and his refusal to accede to his mother's request.

Stephen rejects, or imagines he rejects, all authority. It is in Chapter 4, at the height of his newfound piety, when it is suggested to him that he might have a vocation for the priesthood that the conscious assimilation of experiences into a vision of his future begins. Between this point and the end of the book, in a variety of ways, his sense of himself as an artist with an artist's vision living the life of an artist is consciously formulated.

THE AUTHOR'S VOICE

Objectivity

On first reading, it is easy to be very impressed by Stephen – his intellect, his individuality, his refusal to compromise his principles – and to take him entirely at face value. This, however, would be to miss the irony and humour in Joyce's treatment of him.

Joyce invites us to experience with Stephen, but also to look at him objectively, and it is the genius of his characterisation that we can be involved so intimately in his thoughts and yet see faults to which he is blind, even, at times, perceiving him to be so self-absorbed as to be faintly ridiculous.

We can, for example, understand his feelings when with his father in Cork. Simon Dedalus is full of Blarney, of cliché and posture but Stephen is not exempt from slight disapproval. On the train, he listens 'without sympathy' to his father's account of his youth, stands 'awkwardly' while Dedalus talks to an old acquaintance, 'waiting restlessly' for them to finish, and finds, as his father meets more and more acquaintances leading to greater conversational and alcoholic flow, 'one humiliation succeeded another'. Thus, while what we hear inside Stephen's mind are thoughts such as: 'His mind seemed older than theirs; it shone coldly on their strifes and happiness and regrets like a moon upon a younger earth', what we see is a sulky, bored teenager trying to make himself invisible as he sees his father's behaviour as an embarrassment. We saw this technique operating in *Dubliners*: the accumulation of carefully placed detail which evokes an impression for the careful reader without the conventional intervention of an author's voice.

This irony pervades the book. Stephen is much given to self-dramatisation. In his relationships with women – the real Emma is neglected for romantic images of her – and even in his reaction to the sermons delivered by Father Arnall, his self-imposed regime is a masterpiece of overcompensation. He is so convinced of his own centrality and importance that, at times, he is comic, turning the potential for direct experience or genuine feeling into high flown poetic reflection.

So we are presented with a rounded character as Joyce portrays Stephen warmly and with compassion, understanding what drives him, gently mocking his priggishness and posturing. You will, of course, find many examples of this dual perspective and also note the use of **bathos** to deflate Stephen's more grandiose and eloquent pretensions, a technique to which we will return in the chapter on *Ulysses*.

KEYWORD

Bathos The use of anti-climax for comic effect: building up to a climax which is then undermined by being less than expected.

Stephen returns in *Ulysses*, having been summoned back from Paris by the news of his mother's imminent death and having been at her bedside while she dies. *Ulysses* will put the main character of *Portrait* into the setting of *Dubliners* and allow us to continue following Stephen's emotional and intellectual progress.

✳ ✳ ✳ ✳ SUMMARY ✳ ✳ ✳ ✳

- Portrait is the reworking of an auto-biographical novel begun in a more conventional style.

- It shows how environment affects the development of an artistic personality.

- It is written in the third person, thus giving us a certain distance from Stephen.

- We must be alert to moments in which we are invited to see Stephen in an objective light and to interpret him in terms other than his own.

Major Works III: *Ulysses* 6

BACKGROUND TO ULYSSES

Joyce intended to write a short story for inclusion in *Dubliners* about a Jewish man named Hunter whose wife was rumoured to be unfaithful. The story was never written, but the idea stayed with him and became the germ of what was to become his masterpiece, *Ulysses*, which, with the help of such supporters as Harriet Shaw Weaver and Ezra Pound, began serialisation in *The Little Review* in 1918.

Everyone concerned must have known that there would be difficulties with censorship, and, in February 1921, their fears were justified. *The Little Review* was convicted of publishing obscenity following a trial in New York and serialisation ceased. This ban in America was not to be lifted until 1933.

Despite this, 1921 also saw Joyce announce, in a letter to his friend Frank Budgen, that *Ulysses* was finished. On 22 February 1922 the book's first edition was published by Sylvia Beach's Parisian bookshop 'Shakespeare and Company'. A further edition of 2000 copies was published in England, but copies of a second edition of 500 were seized by the Folkestone Customs Authorities in 1923 and further publication banned.

This situation lasted until 1936, when The Bodley Head brought out a limited edition of 1000 copies, followed by the first unlimited edition in 1937. The book was always surrounded by controversy, however, and its notoriety took a long time to fade: in English public libraries, as late as the 1970s, *Ulysses* was only available on application to the librarian, being deemed too inflammatory for the open shelves.

If the initial 30-odd years of argument about *Ulysses* were over its alleged obscenity and blasphemy, the arguments of the rest have been over textual accuracy and interpretation. As with *Dubliners*, there were lists of amendments to typed sheets or to settings in print, confusions about which copy carried which adjustments, claims and counter-claims about the accuracy or otherwise of different editions. Occasionally, these have received wider attention in the press, but have generally been the concern of scholars, the Joyce estate and advisors of the estate. Argument has, at times, been rancorous.

In 1986 *Ulysses: The Corrected Text*, edited by Hans Walter Gabler, was published in New York and London with an introduction by Joyce's biographer Richard Ellman carrying an account of amendments. Professor Gabler has his detractors, however, and discussion continues:

What has become rather scathingly known as 'The Joyce Industry' continues to grow as his books provide the basis for interpretation after interpretation, theory after theory – and academic thesis after academic thesis. As Joyce himself said:

> 'I've put in so many enigmas and puzzles that it will keep the professors busy for centuries arguing over what I meant, and that's the only way of ensuring one's immortality'.

Used as a preface in Gifford (1988)

He could not, however, have foreseen becoming a tourist attraction, or that, every year on Bloomsday, 16 June, enthusiasts would meet in Dublin to retrace the footsteps of Leopold Bloom, eating food from menus devised from *Ulysses* and listening to concerts of music mentioned in *Ulysses*. In addition to these more light-hearted celebrations, international *James Joyce symposia* have been held since the 1960s in such locations as Paris, Dublin, Zurich and Trieste. A James Joyce Quarterly is published. Contemporary controversies involve the estate's reported objections to readings from *Ulysses* being broadcast over the Internet, and protests over a film, premiered in Dublin in 2000, based on Brenda Maddox's 1988 biography of Nora Joyce.

FIRST READING
Arguments over textual detail are interesting, as are the various interpretations of *Ulysses* offered by different schools of literary criticism,

but they have helped to add to the impression of an impenetrable book accessible only to academics. This is far from the truth.

The aim of this chapter is to give first-time readers, or readers who have given up, sufficient information to deal with some of the book's difficulties without giving so much that the pleasure of independent discovery is dulled. *Ulysses* is a book in which one can become lost. It is, as was its author's intention, a world of its own, ready for exploration and rewarding those who strike their own paths through it. A preliminary reading should:

* make the chronology of the action clear;
* continue the exploration of the development of proto-artist Stephen Dedalus;
* introduce Leopold Bloom and the unparalleled psychological realism with which he is presented;
* reveal the life of a city on one day with such geographical and historical accuracy, and in such detail, that the reader is left with the uncanny sense of having been physically present;
* make clear the main points of the parallel with Homer's *Odyssey*;
* expose patterns of correspondences and symbolism which can be explored at greater depth subsequently;
* introduce and explore themes which run through the work;
* present a dazzling variety of styles of writing, shifts of perspective, wordplay and puzzles as the events of the day are seen from many different angles.

If this sounds too formidable, it must be added that the first-time reader will also laugh aloud and be moved almost to tears.

STRUCTURE: THE HOMERIC PARALLEL

Ulysses is an account of one day in Dublin, 16 June 1904, the activities on that day of Leopold Bloom and his meeting with Stephen Dedalus, artist in embryo. Why, then, is the book named after a hero of Greek legend?

Ulysses was loosely based on Ulysses.

The legend of Ulysses

Odysseus, or 'Ulysses', is the hero of Homer's *Odyssey*. As he returns to his home, Ithaca, and his wife, Penelope, from the Trojan War, his ships are blown off course and he experiences a series of adventures before arriving safely. In his absence, his wife has been beset by a number of suitors who have occupied his palace. His son, Telemachus, has left Ithaca to search for him. At the end of the *Odyssey* father and son are reunited and together they drive out the suitors.

Joyce's *Ulysses* is written in three numbered books. The first and last books each contain three chapters, or episodes, and the central section contains 12. Although neither the books nor the episodes are named, Joyce described these divisions in terms of parallels with the *Odyssey*. The first book corresponds to Telemachus' search for his father, the second to the wanderings of Ulysses and the third to the reuniting of father and son, their triumphant return home and the balance of order being restored to Ithaca.

A COMIC EPIC

Ulysses is often referred to as a '**comic epic**'. In drawing close parallels between the ordinary man as represented by Mr Bloom and the legendary Greek **hero**, Joyce is, in part, having fun with the idea. Much of the humour in *Ulysses* comes from bathos, or anti-climax, in which the serious and important is undermined by comic juxtaposition, and from **parody**, in which the high and lofty are undermined by the lesser. This is reinforced in language and tone: in one episode, for example, events are described from the point of view of a cynical and jaundiced narrator whose sourly colloquial account is punctuated with interpolations in 'high' – or would-be high – styles. Much of *Ulysses* punctures pomposities of attitude or of style and the epic becomes mock, or comic epic.

Humour is not the only reason for the parallel, however. Although there are comic aspects of Mr Bloom's personality, his life and what happens to him during the day, he is too complete a character to be a figure of fun. Here is another example of Joyce's vision and humanity. As in *Portrait*, where we could at once see the world from Stephen's point of view while being aware of his gaucheness and egocentricy, so we can smile at Bloom's eccentricities, be amused by his obsessions, recognise confusions and contradictions in him, while admiring his even-handed compassion, his kindness and innate charity, and understanding his regrets and aspirations. For comic effect, Joyce has reduced the epic to the level of the commonplace, but, perfectly seriously, he has also elevated the commonplace to the level of the epic, showing how we all, in the mundane business of our everyday lives, have something of the heroic in us.

KEYWORDS

Epic Long narrative poem written in lofty style which deals with matters of great importance, celebrating a great theme and glorifying a great hero. A comic epic applies epic principles to lesser matter.

Hero is much more than the modern sense of 'main character'. He is, in the classical sense, a man of superhuman powers, a demigod: a Theseus, a Jason, a Hercules – a Ulysses.

Parody An exaggerated imitation of another piece of writing, usually for comic effect. Parodies abound in the Cyclops episode of *Ulysses*.

STEPHEN DEDALUS

We left Stephen at the end of *Portrait* on his way to Paris, inspired by artistic vision and ready to find his vocation. In the last entry of his journal, he recorded his mother's wish that he 'may learn ... what the heart is and what it feels'. At the same time, he invoked the spirit of Dedalus: 'Old father, old artificer, stand me now and ever in good stead.' This juxtaposition provides a neat summary of Stephen's position: he is a young man whose sense of himself and his own importance is not yet tempered by a real awareness of other people. He is intellect without genuine feeling, passion without compassion, vision without understanding.

At the beginning of *Ulysses*, he has returned from Paris to be at his mother's deathbed. He has refused her dying wish to pray for her, and, despite attempts at justification of one sort or another, he is troubled by his refusal, by memories of her and his treatment of her. He is also virtually estranged from his father, living in a Martello Tower on the beach at Sandycove with his friend Buck Mulligan, 'that Mulligan cad' in the words of Stephen's father. He is without money and any real means, juggling debts working as a teacher in a local school, trying to earn money by selling ideas and articles. During the course of *Ulysses*, he meets Leopold Bloom.

LEOPOLD BLOOM

One of the real pleasures of reading *Ulysses* is meeting Mr Bloom and piecing together the details of his character and his life from the clues given. To begin with, however, Mr Leopold Bloom, called Poldy by his wife, is Jewish, 38 years old and lives at 7 Eccles Street. He is an advertisement canvasser, and is, on this day, working on behalf of Alexander Keyes of the House of Keys, trying to negotiate advertising space in the newspapers. His wife, Marion, known as Molly, was born Marion Tweedy, daughter of Major Tweedy and raised on Gibraltar. The Blooms have a 15-year-old daughter, Milly, who is studying photography at Mullingar. A son, Rudy, had been born 11 years ago, but died 11 days later. Since that time full sexual intercourse has not taken place between the Blooms. Molly is a singer and is about to undertake a concert tour under the management of Hugh 'Blazes' Boylan. On the afternoon of the 16 June, while Bloom is out, Boylan will visit 7 Eccles Street, ostensibly to discuss arrangements for the tour but actually to commit adultery with Mrs Bloom.

CONTRASTING FIGURES

Unlike Stephen, Mr Bloom is not an intellectual, neither does he have any coherent and consistent artistic vision. His mind is full of scraps of general knowledge, half-digested culture, curiosity, random thoughts, impression, sensation and memory inspired by immediate circumstance and sent spinning by association. He is also, however, an immensely humane and compassionate man, at pains to see all sides of every question, always aware of the sensibilities of others. He is at odds with, often buffeted by, but generally triumphant over less charitable and open minds than his.

Important themes are carried by the relationship between Bloom and Stephen and its parallel in Homer. Stephen, the son with no father, having broken away from all the usual authority figures, is brought together with Bloom, the father without a son who has been, in a sense, separated for 11 years from his wife and a complete home. Their meeting is an epiphany after which both may have the means to recognise truths and to use the truths to put their lives in order.

COMPLEMENTING EACH OTHER

The pair complement each other: the self-centred and the self-deprecating; the aloof with the generous; the scientific temperament with the artistic; the intellectual with the intuitive. Have Bloom and Stephen both been enriched by the meeting? Certainly on a level above that of their own perceptions they have and the completeness which together they represent is shown when they are referred to as Stoom and Blephen. There has been speculation about what might be happening on 17 June 1904, on whether or not the significance of the meeting causes a sea-change in Bloom, or whether or not Stephen, having found the substance which his vision lacks, goes away and writes his *Ulysses*. However, speculation is the key word.

THE EPISODES OF ULYSSES

The story of the meeting of Stephen and Bloom and the themes and ideas of the book are carried through 18 episodes, each of which, in a variety of ways, has its parallels in the *Odyssey*. The closeness of these parallels is a source of wonder and a subject for subsequent study. To begin with, it is necessary to show for each episode, what the main events are and how, through character, event and style, the parallels begin.

Telemachus 8.00am The Martello Tower

Stephen reflects upon his life, his situation and his future. He feels used by Buck Mulligan and resolves not to return to the tower. He thinks about his mother's death and there are many implicit and explicit references to the theme of paternity, particularly with reference to Hamlet, the ghost of Hamlet's father and the usurper, Claudius. In Homer, Telemachus leaves Ithaca to search for his father.

Nestor 10.00am School

In Homer, Telemachus asks the sage Nestor for news of his father and is told the story of the Trojan siege. In this episode, Mr Deasy, the schoolmaster for whom Stephen works, talks of European history, the relations between England and Ireland and the Jews as being at the root of the problems. He wishes Stephen to take a letter about the feared foot and mouth epidemic to the editor of the newspaper.

Proteus 11.00am Sandymount Strand

Stephen walks alone on the strand pondering the nature of reality and our lack of ability to see beneath its changing surface: 'ineluctable modality of the visible'. This corresponds in Homer with Menelaus' account of how he wrestled with the sea-god, Proteus, who could change his shape at will and was very difficult to pin down.

WARNING!
It is at this point that many readers new to *Ulysses* give up, but don't. Taken steadily and slowly, bearing in mind that some references will become clearer later in the novel, this beautiful episode is not as difficult for the first-time reader as it appears.

Calypso 8.00am 7 Eccles Street

Leopold Bloom prepares breakfast for his wife. The post brings a card from Bloom's daughter, Milly, and a letter from Boylan. Bloom walks to the butcher's to buy a kidney, returns home, takes his wife breakfast in bed, reads a short story in *Tit-Bits* while relieving himself and then sets out for his day. This episode has its parallel in the seven years which Ulysses spent held in 'amorous captivity' by the nymph Calypso, as Bloom is held in domestic captivity by Molly.

Lotus Eaters 10.00am The Public Baths

In the land of the lotus eaters, Ulysses' men were given the lotus, which left them in a state of drugged inertia, making them forget where they were and what their purpose was. In this episode, the mood is idle, reflective, as Bloom walks the streets observing, remembering, prey to associations and moods. It is, in a way, Bloom's equivalent to Stephen's period of reflection in 'Proteus', and our chance to compare the ways in which their minds work. During this episode of inattention, a misunderstanding about a horse running in the Ascot Gold Cup race begins which will have serious consequences later. The episode finishes with Bloom languishing in the public baths.

Hades 11.00am Glasnevin Cemetery

In Homer, Ulysses visits the underworld and spends time among the dead. Here, Bloom visits the cemetery in the company of other Dublin citizens for the funeral of Paddy Dignam, who died suddenly. Among the company is Simon Dedalus, Stephen's father. It is interesting to see Bloom in the company of Dubliners and to note the differences between them.

Aeolus 12.00 noon Newspaper Offices

Aeolus was the god who helped Ulysses by giving him a bag of winds which would speed his sails. Unfortunately, his men opened the bag prematurely and they were blown off course. When Ulysses asked for more help, he was refused. This episode takes place in the offices of the newspaper to which Stephen has come with Mr Deasy's letter and Bloom has come with the Keyes advertisement. Bloom is at first received favourably, but is rebuffed later. The parallel is to be found in the journalistic style of the episode, which uses just about every known rhetorical style. The association between a newspaper editor and the god of winds is well made.

The Lestrygonians 1.00pm Lunch

The Lestrygonians were a race of cannibals. This episode is dominated by images of food as Bloom, feeling hungry, visits Davy Byrnes' for lunch, only to be repelled by the sights and sounds of the diners. There is much reminiscing about Molly and a meeting with an old flame, Josie Breen. The misunderstanding about the horse gathers momentum. At the end of the episode a near encounter with Boylan sends him into the museum for refuge.

Scylla and Charybdis 2.00pm Library

In Homer, Ulysses had to steer a course between a many-headed monster, Scylla, and a whirlpool, Charybdis. This episode focuses upon Stephen in discussion with his peers, mirroring Bloom's conversation with his contemporaries in Hades. They are exploring Stephen's Shakespearian theories, among other issues. Bloom is seen picking his way carefully between the protagonists as, on the one side, barbs of argument are fired, and, on the other, whirlpool depths are exposed. Again, Bloom and Stephen are nearly brought together.

ANOTHER WARNING!

First-time readers who survive Proteus sometimes founder here. Again, careful reading, perhaps supplemented by some knowledge of the life of Shakespeare and the plot of Hamlet will help.

Wandering Rocks 3.00pm Dublin Streets

This episode is divided into 19 short sections which give glimpses of most of the characters as they move through the city. A white arm throwing coins from a window to a beggar is Molly; a dark back at a bookstall is Bloom; a straw hat shining in the sun is Boylan. These glimpses are threaded together by a journey across Dublin being made by Father Conmee in one direction and the Earl of Dudley in another. This episode was composed with meticulous attention to timing, with Joyce using a map and a clock to ensure that the synchronicity was correct. In Homer, wandering rocks were a danger to navigation.

The Sirens 4.00pm The Ormond Hotel

The Sirens were temptresses who lured sailors to their deaths with the beauty of their song and this remarkable episode is written as a piece of music, beginning with an overture in which all the sounds of the episode are heard. It contains musical devices in the same way that Aeolus contained rhetorical devices. Bloom, eating a late lunch in the back room, is moved emotionally by the singing of drinkers in the bar, including Simon Dedalus, particularly since, during this time, Boylan leaves the bar for his meeting with Molly. The sirens themselves are represented by the two barmaids, Misses Kennedy and Douce, 'bronze by gold'.

Cyclops 5.00pm Barney Kiernan's

Polyphemus was the Cyclops, a one-eyed giant who intends to eat Ulysses and his sailors. Ulysses escapes by blinding him. In this episode, Cyclops is represented by The Citizen, an old Irish Nationalist who occupies his seat in the pub talking politics and rebellion. He is one-eyed in the sense that he only sees one point of view and the episode is full of 'one-eyed' imagery. Bloom visits the pub in order to take up a collection for Paddy Dignam's widow and finds himself embroiled in argument with The Citizen and his companions which is fuelled as the misunderstanding concerning the horse reaches its climax. The Cyclops is, metaphorically, blinded by Bloom's even-handedness and ability to see both sides. The passage is narrated by an anonymous drinker of unparalleled cynicism and lack of charity. His sour version of events interpolated with inflated and hyperbolic language heightens the comic effect.

Nausicaa 8.00pm The Rocks on Sandymount Strand

Ulysses was washed up on the island of Phaecia and cared for by the king's daughter, Nausicaa. Here, Bloom, after escaping from The Citizen, takes a brief respite while watching Gerty McDowell, a young girl, as she sits on the rocks. The first part of the episode is narrated from Gerty's point of view in the sentimental, sickly style of a romantic novelette. In a feast of self-dramatisation and romantic clichés, she sees the 'dark stranger' watching her, partly concealed by the rocks, and weaves him into her fantasy. As she leans further back, revealing her underclothes, Bloom masturbates, and his climax coincides with the climaxes of a mass taking place in a church in Howth and a firework display across the strand.

Oxen of the Sun 10.00pm Holles Street Maternity Hospital

This episode brings Bloom and Stephen together. Bloom is enquiring after Mrs Purefoy, who has been three days in labour. Stephen is drinking with medical students and friends. The oxen of the sun were sacred beasts sacrilegiously slaughtered by Odysseus' men. Here, the sacrament of birth is desecrated by the drunken students and their bawdy, irreverent talk. The period of gestation is mirrored in the development of the English language, the episode beginning with an incantation, progressing through a Latinate structure, Anglo-Saxon rhythms and so on through the centuries.

Circe 12.00 midnight Nighttown

The revellers have left the hospital for more drink and then move into Nighttown, Dublin's red light area. Bloom, worried about Stephen, follows and, eventually, rescues him from a beating at the hands of two British soldiers. Circe was the enchantress who turned Ulysses' men into swine, and here every image, passing reference, unconscious desire, is brought up, inflated to nightmare proportions and personified. Secret indiscretions and yearnings are exposed and the dead come back to life. The episode is written as a script, with stage directions and sound effects. It is difficult and much of it has not been explained even by assiduous scholarship, but the wildness of the imagery is spectacular.

Eumaeus 1.00pm The Cabman's Shelter

When Ulysses returned to Ithaca disguised as a beggar, he enters the hut of the swineherd Eumaeus where he is reunited with Telemachus. Stephen's companions have deserted him and it is left to Bloom to dust him off and get him to safety. They sit in the cabman's shelter talking to each other and to the assortment of people sitting there, including an old sailor who tells tall stories of the sea. The episode is full of images of wandering and return. The style of the episode reflects the lateness of the hour, Bloom's tiredness and Stephen's befuddled state in long, rambling, sometimes inconclusive sentences and in conversations which are frequently at cross purposes.

Ithaca 2.00am 7 Eccles Street

Ulysses returned home and vanquished his rivals. Bloom, having learnt that Stephen has nowhere to go, invites him to stay the night. This episode, apparently Joyce's favourite, is written in what he called a 'mathematical catechism', in which all sentiment and subjectivity is stripped away and, in a series of questions and answers, Stephen and Bloom's walk back, their conversation, aspects of their pasts, and so on, are given with scientific objectivity. Bloom and Stephen are thus placed side by side and found to be 'similar in their differences'.

Penelope Bed

Stephen has left and Bloom has climbed into bed beside his wife. She asks him about his day and then, as he sleeps, we enter her mind. This is the most celebrated episode of the book. In an otherwise unpunctuated eight sentences, Molly's stream of consciousness, fast, bawdy, hilarious, touching, tumbles over her day, her life, her hopes, her past and her marriage, finishing with one of the most glorious affirmations in all literature. The liquid flow of her thoughts is a return to the flow of life after the aridity of the previous two episodes' styles, and is halted twice, appropriately, by the corresponding physical flows of urine and menstruation.

STREAM OF CONSCIOUSNESS

We saw in *Dubliners* that there was no recognisable authorial voice as we find in, say, Dickens or Trollope, but that we were presented with characters and events obliquely, from perspectives which enabled us to make judgements for ourselves. In *Portrait*, we saw this determination to leave the reader independent

> **KEYTERM**
>
> Stream of consciousness Writing which attempts to reproduce exactly and in real time the apparently random sequences of thought which stream through our minds.

taken further as we moved seamlessly from external description and narrative into Stephen's thoughts and subjective experiences. In *Ulysses*, Joyce removes himself even further. Some of the episodes are narrated from a recognisable point of view – the anonymous drinker and Gerty McDowell, for example: still others in a deliberately impersonal manner – the newspaper, the script, the catechism – but for much of the time we are directly inside the heads of Stephen, Bloom and Molly. This technique is known as **stream of consciousness**.

The funeral scene

This technique means that we must be alert. Sometimes the train of thought is obvious. At a funeral, Bloom watches the horse which has drawn the carriage bearing the coffin and muses:

> Do they know what they cart out here every day? Must be twenty or thirty funerals every day. Then Mount Jerome for the Protestants. Funerals all over the world everywhere every minute. Shovelling them under by the cartload doublequick. Thousands every hour. Too many in the world.

At the Hotel Ormond

At other times Joyce's use of stream of consciousness techniques make his writing much harder to follow. For example, as Bloom sits in the dining area of the Ormond Hotel listening to the heart-tugging songs from the bar he thinks:

Jiggedy jingle jaunty jaunty.

Only the harp. Lovely gold glowering light. Girl touched it. Poop of a lovely. Gravy's rather good fit for a. Golden ship Erin. The harp that once or twice. Cool hands. Ben Howth, the rhododendrons. We are their harps. I. He. Old. Young.

There is a wealth of references here which the reader may not yet be in a position to interpret. What is happening is this: the sound of Boylan's jaunting car as he drives towards Molly connects in Bloom's head with the jingling of the bed-quoits as Molly turned over in bed that morning for her breakfast. That, and the sound of the piano from the bar, remind him of an evening with Molly at the theatre, and this will be returned to later in this episode and in Molly's monologue.

He thinks of the cool hands of the harpist and the harp itself as the prow of a ship. He is temporarily distracted by the quality of the food, but the thought 'fit for a' stops before the word 'king', thus sliding neatly into images of Erin's kings via the harp and thence to memories of happy times with Molly on Ben Howth, her cool hands, and the flowers which lead Bloom to think of how women can play men as harpists play harps. He finishes with a poignant reflection on the respective ages of himself and Boylan. The references to the harp and Ireland help continue the themes of betrayal, exile and usurpation.

As we progress through the book we must be alert to echoes and repetitions, to pick up slight clues and remember them. We must gather hints and images, often from different perspectives, which will accumulate into a complete picture.

FOLLOWING THREADS

This guide has chosen to concentrate on the surface with narrative, character and setting because, although *Ulysses* is a book which is teeming with ideas, Joyce chose not to write it as a philosophical essay, but as a novel. *Ulysses* is not an allegory with fixed correspondences whose purpose is to teach or make a point, as, for example *Pilgrim's Progress* or *Animal Farm*. Joyce, remember, does not aim to teach, but to reveal, and what he reveals is a world of infinite connectedness in which everything, however separate it seems, impinges on the existence of everything else.

Themes and correspondences

Themes are carried mercurially through the book by the unlikeliest of vessels and correspondences are protean: they cannot be pinned down and simplified. In the main theme of the nature of paternity, the parallels between Stephen/Bloom and Ulysses/Telemachus is the main correspondence, but the theme is also explored via Shakespeare and Hamlet and the Holy Family. Bloom is a Dubliner, but also an exile, identified at times with the Jewishness which makes him so and at other times with Ireland usurped by a foreign power as Bloom has been temporarily usurped by Boylan. Correspondences are strengthened by symbols: Nelson's Pillar, symbol of the usurper's power, is stuck in the middle of Dublin as Boylan's penis is stuck in the middle of Molly. Although the theme of a betrayed and usurped country runs through the book, however, the reader would be foolish to attribute a stance, in the sense of a fixed political view. Irish Nationalism, remember, is represented by The Citizen, and Ireland is 'the old sow who eats her farrow'. The reader's mind must remain open and try not to follow false trails along narrow lines.

You will find, however, that this is not a book which you will open at the first page and read straight through until you come to the last. You will spend a great deal of time flicking backwards with amusement to check a reference or with delight to confirm a discovery. You will want to trace references to keys, bars of soap, horses, tins of potted meat and so on, to trace the novel's rich symbolism.

FOR A FIRST READING

On a first reading, it is almost impossible not to want to follow threads. Some suggestions to follow include:

* Bloom's secretive and slightly voyeuristic sexuality is revealed in different ways throughout the book, from furtive memories to watching women in the street, from his secret correspondence with Martha under the pseudonym of Henry Flower to Gerty McDowell, and the grotesqueness of the Circe episode when all his sexual sins, real and imagined, are presented to him in grossly inflated forms.

* Mr Bloom's practicality, his scientific turn of mind is well worth following. He is forever explaining natural phenomena, wondering about how things work, speculating upon costs and profits.

* Bloom's reactions to and thoughts about Boylan and Molly. The way in which Joyce portrays Bloom's mind as trying to turn aside from the thought whenever it presents itself, as he physically tries to avoid seeing Boylan in the street, has great psychological realism and is both moving and amusing. The Freudian slips, the double-entendres which reveal his real state of mind are beautifully handled.

* The climate of vague anti-Jewishness in which Bloom has to move is suggested, explicitly through the words of Deasy or Haines and implicitly in the actions and attitudes of people around Bloom. Joyce presents a perfectly drawn example of what we now would call institutional racism and shows us what it is like to be considered a stranger in a land which you consider home.

There is so much to enjoy, now and later: the dazzling wordplay, the historical perspectives, the philosophical and religious explorations which have exercised so many interpreters and contributed to discussion about this most multi-faceted of all works of fiction.

If you have read *Portrait*, you will be given information about Stephen's life between the finish of that book and the 16th June 1904 in the first three episodes of *Ulysses* by means of Stephen's memory, his conversation with Mulligan and the situations in which we are shown him. We are, however, thrown into the middle of the lives of Mr and Mrs Bloom: the details of their lives prior to the preparation of breakfast on that morning come to us over the course of the day in flashback. It is interesting as we read to pick up clues, references, allusions and try to get a sense of the lives of Leopold and Molly as they might be written in conventional, linear, biographical style. The accumulation of detail is not only fascinating in its own right, but will certainly help to reinforce your sense of wonder at Joyce's artistic vision and the structure of the book as a whole.

✳ ✳ ✳ ✳SUMMARY ✳ ✳ ✳ ✳

- *Ulysses* is an account of one day in the life of Leopold Bloom.

- It is organised into 18 episodes, each corresponding to an episode in Homer's *Odyssey*.

- The Homeric parallels establish the theme of paternity which is explored in many ways.

- Much of the novel is written using stream of consciousness techniques.

- Symbols, themes, ideas, run through the novel and add to its richness.

- The novel presents a 'God's-eye' view of a world in which everything is interconnected.

Contemporary Critical Approaches

7

It is a measure of how different Joyce's writing was from what had gone before him that even those who might have known him best were so confounded as to be suspicious. His wife, as is well known, refused to read *Ulysses*, finding it obscene. This is possibly because she recognised aspects of herself in such characters as Bella Cohen, the brothel keeper, and, primarily, Molly Bloom. As Brenda Maddox says in her (1988) biography *Nora*:

> Nora's aversion to the book could...have sprung from recognition. Too many of the lines were her own.
>
> p. 273

WHO'S MOLLY?

AN ELABORATE JOKE

Joyce was, apparently, amused by his wife's reaction, and it was certainly his sense of humour that made his brother Stanislaus suspicious of early drafts of fragments of *Finnegans Wake*. In a letter to Joyce Stanislaus wrote that he had received an instalment and was suspicious that his brother was merely staging an elaborate hoax.

The suspicion that Joyce was playing some kind of joke upon the literati was to be voiced later by someone else who could claim to have known Joyce well: Oliver St John Gogarty had been a great friend of Joyce in Dublin before Joyce's departure for Europe. When they met, Gogarty was a student and was later to become a famous surgeon and poet. They became friends, drinking companions and, for a while, shared unconventional accommodation – a Martello Tower at Sandycove. The two men later fell out very badly and Gogarty's view of Joyce's success remained very critical. Gogarty too accused Joyce of having perpetrated a gigantic hoax and pictured him trapped: finding himself unexpectedly taken seriously by duped and gullible, chiefly American, critics.

Of course, Gogarty's enmity had been aroused by his representation in *Ulysses* as Buck Mulligan but it remains interesting that it is the charge of fraud which two men who knew him, one kindly disposed towards him, the other less so, should level.

INITIAL REACTIONS TO DUBLINERS AND PORTRAIT

We have seen the difficulties which Joyce experienced in having *Dubliners* published as he wished and the string of compromises which he had to make to conventional decency and the nervousness of printers and publishers. Three of the stories had been published in the 1904 *Irish Homestead*, but they were not well received. To readers used to the traditions established in the nineteenth-century novel, they seemed to lack plot and focus, to be written in a flat, unengaging style and to be rather low in subject matter with nothing uplifting from which a moral truth may be derived. Ideas and techniques which Joyce shared with the

Irish writer George Moore and from de Maupassant, Flaubert, Zola, Chekhov and, of course, Ibsen, were not then common currency and readers were in general mystified and indifferent.

Reviewers commented on the strong sense of place and the feel of the city which *Dubliners* so brilliantly conveys and on the quality of the writing, the sense of style. Some identify the humour, but find it underscored by morbidity, pessimism or even the power of evil. A full review appeared in the *New Statesman* by Gerald Gould which linked Joyce's name with that of Gorky and acknowledged him as a man of genius. Gould also identified the relationship between the author, his material and his reader but saw it again as something morbid. Gould recognised the unparalleled realism of Joyce's recording of ordinary conversation. He also joined other, less perceptive, reviewers in wishing that Joyce would elevate his sights and not waste his genius upon the ordinary, which rather missed the point.

Joyce's powerful allies

Joyce, however, was to gain some powerful allies. W.B. Yeats had admired the collection of poems, *Chamber Music* and also thought that *Dubliners* showed great promise. He drew Joyce to the attention of Ezra Pound, who saw, as did later French reviewers, the tradition from which Joyce had drawn and whose tenets he was to extend so dramatically. Pound recognised that Joyce 'gives the thing as it is', without sentimentality or hidden agenda. He recognised the characterisation of individuals rather than types, the paring down of details. Crucially, he recognised that:

> The author is quite capable of dealing with things about him, and dealing directly, yet these details do not engross him, he is capable of getting at the universal element beneath.

Ezra Pound, *Dubliners and Mr. James Joyce*, Egoist 15 July 1914, quoted in
Deming (1970), p. 67

Ezra Pound's influence and admiration were to be invaluable to Joyce. It was Pound who persuaded Harriet Shaw Weaver, owner of the modernist review *The Egoist* to begin to run *Portrait* as a serial in 1914 and the book appeared in a single volume in 1916, open to general review and criticism.

Beautiful but dirty

Again, critics and reviewers were torn between admiration for the brilliance of the style with what they saw as the sordidness of the content. A reader's report for the publisher Duckworth from 1916 shows how thoroughly the work was misunderstood. Edward Garnett, a novelist and playwright himself, had, as a publisher's reader, offered encouragement to such authors as Forster, Conrad and Lawrence, but even he found Joyce too much. He thought the book showed both a lack of editing and of restraint. Another review saw *Portrait* astonishingly powerful but also extraordinarily dirty. Others saw it as clever but sordid, appreciating the beauty but being revolted by moments of coarseness.

Again, a review in the *New Republic* by Francis Hackett complained that Joyce had not given any thought to plot and considered that its peculiar narrative method made the book less clear. The reviewer from the *Guardian*, however, thought that the book's apparent formlessness should not be held against it.

Pound continued to support, giving more insight to Joyce's methods and intentions than the uninvolved reviewer could hope to: Pound linked Joyce to Flaubert and noted his realism. Other important writers were adding their voices. H.G. Wells noted that one could believe in Stephen Dedalus as one believed in few characters in fiction. He particularly admired the Christmas dinner episode in which Parnell was discussed, but saw 'hate, a cant cultivated to the pitch of monomania' levelled at the English. (review, *Nation*, 24 February 1917, quoted in Deming, op cit, p. 88). Six years later the American, Hart Crane, was to identify in *Portrait* a sense of charity: a completely opposing view of the same text.

This small selection from contemporary reviews, some from eminent writers, some from ordinary reviewers, give an indication of the confusion which Joyce's writing caused. This was nothing, however, when placed beside what was to come. Hart Crane wrote his praise of Joyce while waiting to read *Ulysses*. Virginia Woolf had praised *Portrait* in 1919, but noted the imminence of 'what promises to be a far more interesting work'. *Ulysses* was being serialised in *The Little Review*.

INITIAL REACTIONS TO ULYSSES

As *Ulysses* began serialisation in 1918, a new edition of *Portrait* was published and Joyce was arousing much interest and excitement. A letter from Yeats dated 1918 catches the spirit of anticipation surrounding *Ulysses*:

> I think him a most remarkable man, and his new story in *The Little Review* looks like becoming the best work he has done. It is an entirely new thing – neither what the eye sees nor the ear hears, but what the rambling mind thinks and imagines from moment to moment. He has certainly surpassed in intensity any novelist of our time.
>
> Letter to John Quinn 23 July 1918, quoted in Deming, op cit p. 172

It seems to be the stream of consciousness technique which caught the imagination of early readers of the serial. Certainly, few would have had any inkling of the larger picture, the symbolic coherence, the parallels, the sweep and immense ambition of the author's vision. In 1921 serialisation was stopped following the charge of obscenity, but in 1922 *Ulysses* first appeared in book form.

Many of the early reviews and reactions are anthologised in an excellent two-volume compilation edited by Robert H. Deming called *James Joyce: The Critical Heritage* and browsing through it is fascinating and often very funny. There is a sense of complete mystification from some reviewers who cover their confusions with words such as 'boring', 'turgid', 'tiresome' and, more honestly, 'incomprehensible' which recur quite frequently.

There is also the sense of reviewers and literary men standing up for real books against the tide of experimental nonsense designed to delude the so-called intellectuals. Joyce was again accused of perpetrating a hoax.

Ulysses was not immediately recognised for the work it was.

Shane Leslie, in the *Quarterly Review* of 1922, suggested that a gigantic effort had been made to fool the world of readers. Later, Joyce was to say to Frank Budgen that the only kind of critic he resented was 'the kind that affects to believe that I am writing with my tongue in my cheek' (Budgen (1972), p. 108).

Many of the reviews expressed outrage. In one Joyce was described as a perverted lunatic and in another in the *Daily Express*, the reviewer runs the gamut of indignant disgust and sums his view up with a magnificent simile:

> Reading Mr. Joyce is like making an excursion into Bolshevik Russia: all standards go by the board.
>
> *Daily Express*, 25 March 1922, quoted in Deming, op cit p. 191

OUTRAGE AND INSIGHT

Amid the outrage, however, there was some insight. Two or three reviewers call the book 'unmoral', which is true: to accuse the book of immorality is to accuse it of taking a moral stance, and Joyce does not do that: he presents, we observe. Other reviewers of this period note the parallel with the Greek Odysseus and the notion of Bloom as 'Everyman'.

The first serious and lengthy consideration of Joyce's writing came in 1922 from Valery Larbaud, the French writer and critic. He had discussed the books with Joyce, and therefore wrote with some authority. His long article 'James Joyce' appeared in the *Nouvelle Revue Française* and was the first to treat Joyce's books as a whole, to see the unity which we now take for granted. Other contemporary essays stressed and explored different facets of *Ulysses*: T.S. Eliot was interested in the mythical aspects of the book, the Homeric parallels and the pattern of symbolism. Ezra Pound compared Joyce to Flaubert and pursued the theme of father and son. For Virginia Woolf, who had admired *Portrait* and waited eagerly for *Ulysses*, however, the book was redolent of 'a queasy undergradulate scratching his pimples', and D.H. Lawrence thought Molly's monologue to be 'the dirtiest, most indecent, obscene thing ever written' . (Woolf quoted in Ellman, op cit, p. 528; Lawrence quoted in Ellman, op cit p. 615).

Understanding

Joyce stayed away from the controversy, but, as a clever publicist, allowed details of his scheme for *Ulysses* to issue piecemeal, through chosen critics and friends. Of the three books on Joyce and particularly on *Ulysses*, which most served to shape knowledge and understanding, two were written by friends and associates of the author. Stuart Gilbert's *James Joyce's Ulysses* appeared in 1930, Frank Budgen's *James Joyce and the Making of Ulysses* in 1934. The definitive biography, *James Joyce* by Richard Ellman, was published in 1959.

GILBERT REVEALS THE STRUCTURE

Gilbert revealed fully, for the first time, how complex was the structure of *Ulysses* and how rich was the variety of structures, patterns of symbols and use of language. Above all, critics who complained that the book lacked cohesion, that it was a leg-pull, that it was a jumble of styles and disconnected content, were shown that the book had a deliberately and finely worked out unity: that nothing in it was superfluous or unnecessary. The study consists of two parts.

In the first, there are introductory essays which address issues of biography, of Homeric parallel, of the political and historical background to *Ulysses* and some of the main themes. There is a chart showing, for the first time to the general reader and most critics, the working names of the episodes, revealing the broad Homeric parallel. The chart also assigns to each episode a scene and an hour of the day, thus making the chronological progression of Bloom's odyssey clear. More amazingly, however, the chart also allocates to each episode a governing art, symbol and 'technic', or narrative style. It showed that the last 15 episodes were each also governed by an organ of the body, while certain episodes were assigned dominating colours.

The second part of Gilbert's study was called 'The Episodes' and it consisted of 18 chapters, each one dealing with a separate episode of *Ulysses*, taking the reader through it in detail, with extensive quotations and illustrations, commenting fully upon meaning and technique.

BUDGEN'S INSIGHTS INTO CHARACTER

Frank Budgen's book is a much more relaxed and leisurely affair. Budgen was a painter, working at the British Consulate in Zurich in 1918 when he met Joyce. They became friends and Joyce discussed many aspects of *Ulysses* with him over the years. *James Joyce and the Making of Ulysses* is, in part, an account of Budgen's conversations with Joyce and, in part, an account of the events of the novel.

Budgen's style is direct and personal, and his warmth and interest are communicated clearly: the book's enthusiasm is infectious, and Budgen takes the role of an intelligent reader who is not particularly literary (although several of his reported conversations with Joyce give the lie to that). His book is clearly intended for the lay reader rather than the academic, and it concentrates upon events, characters and ideas rather than technique and symbol.

There are 14 chapters in the book. The first two describe how the author first met Joyce, conversations with Mr and Mrs Joyce, an account of how their friendship grew and a description of contemporary Zurich. The fourteenth chapter looks at what was to become *Finnegans Wake*, then known as 'Work in Progress'. The intervening 11 chapters follow the episodes of *Ulysses*, describing what happens in them and generally commenting upon characters and illustrating the account with apparently verbatim discussions with Joyce on Joyce's thoughts. An interesting feature is Budgen's – and, by extension, Joyce's – immensely positive view of characters about whom future commentators express, and assume that Joyce intended them to feel, ambivalence.

The 'Nestor' episode introduces Mr Deasy, the schoolteacher, who seems to modern eyes a prime example of Joyce's ironic technique, yet Budgen appears to take him at face value describing him as a 'shrewd, brave old man' with whom Stephen shares an 'instinctive sympathy' (Budgen, op cit, pp. 45–6).

The Making of Ulysses is a delightful book. Budgen is an erudite and very charming guide and commentator. Part of his function seems to be that of putting a human face on to a fearsome intellect, and the frequent pictures of Joyce's eyes twinkling with sardonic humour or Joyce laughing aloud as he reads passages from his work, certainly do that. Budgen's own observations are always interesting. They serve to remind us that, despite the formidable technique and complex plan, *Ulysses* is 'never solemn ... often fantastically comic ... amoral and philosophically humane, [but] always serious' (Budgen, op cit p. 72). Richard Ellman's biography was not to appear for another 25 years after the publication of Gilbert, but, within that time, new, focused, scientific schools of literary criticism had been founded.

PRACTICAL AND NEW CRITICISM

The name most associated with practical criticism is that of F.R. Leavis who, as a probationary lecturer at Cambridge in the late 1920s, suffered rebuke for introducing the banned *Ulysses* to his students. He and his wife, Q.D. Leavis, began a periodical called *Scrutiny* which sought to redefine the practice of literary criticism along more analytical lines by means of 'close reading'. It was meant to, and did, gain English recognition as an academic discipline.

Practical criticism operated upon scientific lines, taking books apart and studying the elements of characterisation, diction, style, plot, setting and so on, which comprised them, making judgements on the basis not of the way in which the author lived his or her life, not on the social and historical background against which the writer worked, but on the merits or demerits of the text itself. This led Leavis and his colleagues to redefine the canon of English literature in a way that profoundly affected what was read at universities for the next few generations. The Victorians, for example, were given a back seat, while modern writers such as T.S. Eliot, Gerard Manley Hopkins and D.H. Lawrence were argued for. Leavis wrote of a 'Great Tradition' of English prose fiction comprising such writers as Jane Austen, George Eliot, Conrad, Henry James and D.H. Lawrence as authors whose books were capable of providing moral education, of uplifting and expanding experience. In the hands of great writers, to study literature was to study life, but the focus must be the text itself, not the life of the writer or the circumstances in which the writer lived. Many years of university, college, secondary school, examination syllabuses and teaching have been constructed upon these principles and it is due to such as Leavis and Richards that English still occupies, even in our electronic, technological and computerised age, its central position in the country's educational system.

POETRY AS A MEANS OF REDEMPTION

Richards was a teacher and critic who taught at Cambridge and later continued a highly successful career at Harvard. He conducted experiments on how people read and formed literary judgements, giving undergraduates a range of poetry to read without any information about who wrote it. His conclusion was that our judgements about literature were highly subjective. For Richards, the model for the acquisition of real knowledge was scientific, but scientific inquiry had nothing emotional or spiritual in it. The study of poetry fills the gap left by the mythological and the religious in a world dominated by scientific and technological thought. 'Poetry is capable of saving us,' he wrote, 'it is a perfectly possible means of overcoming chaos' (quoted in Eagleton (1983), p. 45).

A poem, a work of literature, was an organic whole, an object in itself, to be studied and analysed: the intentions of the author, the life of the author, the readers' responses, social and historical factors were, at most, secondary considerations.

FURTHER CRITICAL STUDIES

In the meantime, critics were beginning to agree that Joyce was writing more in a European literary tradition rather than an English tradition. These critics were mainly French, such as Larbaud, or American, such as Edmund Wilson. In 1941, Harry Levin's *James Joyce: A Critical Introduction* appeared. It took *Portrait* as autobiography, and had much to say about Joyce's symbolism. Critical discussion into the 1950s was concerned mainly with searching for Joyce's sources, unravelling strands of symbolism, analysing structure and linguistic devices and focusing on Stephen, both as a character, and as a representation of Joyce himself. In 1956, *Joyce: the Man, The Work and The Reputation* by Richard Kain and Marvin Magalaner appeared, dealing with the question of Joyce's autobiography by referring to *Ulysses, Portrait*, unpublished letters and the first draft of *Portrait, Stephen Hero*, which, by then, had appeared in print. In the 1950s, the critic William York Tindall wrote *James Joyce: His Way of Interpreting the Modern World*, to be followed in 1959 by *A Reader's Guide*, in which, among other issues, he returns to the question of Stephen as Joyce. His book appeared, however, in the same year as the ground-breaking biography, *James Joyce*, by Richard Ellman.

Ellman's biographical study

Richard Ellman was an American academic and critic who had been educated at Yale. He became established as an important critical voice with his book *Yeats: The Man and the Mask*, published in 1948. His 900-page biography of Joyce was hailed as a new direction for literary biography: it is an exhaustively researched account of Joyce's life which also shows and gives evidence for the close connections between the details of Joyce's life and those of Stephen Dedalus. It may have been irrelevant for a Leavisite critic how much of Dickens was in the character and life of, say, David Copperfield, but for a proper appreciation of Joyce, whose subject is the creation of a writer, the relationship between the portrait of an artist and the life of the artist is of considerable importance.

The next chapter will trace the directions in which this melding of autobiography and fiction led and how the idea of the unity of Joyce's work and life has taken hold, as well as looking at how some of the modern schools of literary criticism, or 'theory', treat James Joyce.

✳ ✳ ✳ ✳ SUMMARY ✳ ✳ ✳ ✳

- All three books were generally misunderstood at first.

- *Ulysses* particularly was seen as obscene, confusing or, at worst, as a gigantic hoax.

- Continental critics were more receptive and understanding than the British.

- As more was learned about Joyce's intentions, organisation and schemes, critics began to see the books differently and appreciation grew.

- Academic studies and critical examinations grew during the 1950s and 1960s.

- Leavis did not place Joyce in the 'Great Tradition', but saw him as part of an aberrant strain.

Modern Critical Approaches 8

The radical changes in literary criticism over the course of the past 30 years have seen many different approaches to Joyce. Practical and new criticism, with its emphasis upon the purity of the written word, uncontaminated by social, historical, political or biographical conditions, gave way to a variety of methods of interpreting texts. Note the phrase 'interpreting texts' rather than 'reading books': we have moved from the allegedly dilettante 'old school', which did, after all, include Hazlitt and Johnson, in which criticism was largely a matter of the good taste and the sound judgement of the critic, through Leavis and Richards, to a study of literature which resembles less an aesthetic than a scientific exploration. Literary criticism, in the Johnsonian and even the Leavisite sense has been superseded by the range of schools of thought known simply as 'theory'.

THEORY

These different schools of criticism include the **structuralist** and post-structuralist, the feminist, the Marxist, the psychoanalytic, the new historicist, the reader-response school, and so on. The wonder of Joyce is that he managed to anticipate most of them – one of the reasons

> **KEYWORD**
>
> Structuralism The idea that all elements of human culture can be understood as a system of signs.

why he was so misunderstood by his contemporary critics was that he was operating outside their terms of reference: what he wrote could not be addressed in the conventional language of literary criticism as they understood it, hence the cries of bewilderment about plotlessness or the confusion of being moved willy-nilly inside a character's mind and outside again without any clear indication of which was which. Leavis recognised this when he said that Joyce's influence was seen 'in a line of writers to which there is no parallel issuing from Lawrence'.

A brief and simple look at the central tenets of some of these schools will illustrate the means by which Joyce anticipated them.

Structuralist criticism

Structuralist criticism seeks to identify 'codes' which give meanings to phenomena such as texts: Stephen Dedalus, on Sandymount Strand, pondered the 'ineluctable modality of the visible' and the reality beneath the shifting surface of things. The structuralist emphasis upon signifiers and signified comes to mind as Stephen walks along Sandymount Strand and, looking at the scene around him, muses: 'Signatures of all things I am here to read.'

Early structuralist critics, such as Northrop Frye, saw literature as a closed system, feeding off itself, seen best in relation to other works of literature, creating its own myths. *Ulysses* makes literary history central in the identification of Bloom so closely with his mythological predecessor; in the Shakespearian themes which pervade; and, of course, in the 'Oxen of the Sun' episode in which the stages of embryonic development undergone by the Purefoy baby are paralleled in the variety of literary styles adopted. These move, in chronological sequence, from the alliterative style of Anglo-Saxon verse through the literary styles of the centuries, finishing in a sort of cosmopolitan early twentieth-century slang.

Feminist criticism

Feminist criticism approaches literature from a gender viewpoint. It questions the portrayal of women, and the effects of the portrayal of women, in a field which has been dominated by men. Joyce, however, closes *Ulysses* with an uninterrupted 30-plus page internal monologue given by his main woman character. During the course of this monologue, she gives a new perspective to much of what we have heard before, giving us a picture of herself not known to Leopold and a portrait of Leopold not known either to himself or his friends.

Psychoanalytical criticism

Psychoanalytical criticism analyses literature in terms of the unconscious mind: the unconscious mind is to the fore in *Ulysses* and no bones are made about the relationship between author and character.

Stream of consciousness allows the reader inside the mind of the character in an unprecedented way and the manifestation of the unconscious in the actions and speech of character is fully explored.

New historicism

New historicism explores the social, political and historical contexts within which texts are written and read: Joyce places contemporary politics, social milieus and the history of Ireland at the centre of his books and shows the significance of historical action, in this case, the disgrace and death of Parnell, in the lives of his characters.

Above all, however, the crippling injunction upon literature to be 'morally uplifting' has, by and large, been left behind. The distinction between 'high' and 'low' has gone, or, at least, become very blurred. Leavis replied to those who praised Henry Fielding's 'subtlety of organisation' that such qualities were not possible 'without richer material to organise ...

> **KEYWORDS**
>
> New historicism a criticism which seeks to see works of literature in their historical and cultural contexts.
>
> Feminist criticism looks at the presentation of women, ways in which masculine ideology is carried in texts and the undervaluing of woman writers. More recently the term has become broader, studying all texts from a female perspective and looking at the relationships between men and women in the light of the gender debate.

than Fielding has to offer'. This point of view could have been applied by contemporary critics of Joyce, who found his material sordid and his characters unworthy of our attention. Joyce's detachment, his irony, his refusal to indulge us with easy value judgements about his characters and their behaviour, his sense of the unity between artist and environment, his conscious use of the details of his own life in his fiction, and, above all, his placement of the ordinary man at the centre of the universe, make him a quintessentially modern writer.

JOYCE AND FEMINIST CRITICISM

There are as many different views of Joyce in **feminist criticism** as there are in any other. There are pro-Joyceans and anti-Joyceans. The pro-Joyceans see, for example, Molly Bloom as a proto-feminist undermining male authority. The anti-Joyceans see her as a slovenly, self-absorbed, ignorant, vain and insulting stereotype. Some see women in Joyce excluded from cultural life, as exemplified in Molly's ignorance – 'O, rocks! Tell us in plain words.' Others see in Stephen's resentment of his dependency on the language of the usurper, English, a parallel with feminist resentment of a language structure which stresses a male view of the world.

Joyce, as might be expected, remains contradictory. Widely quoted is his remark to Mary Colum, stating that he hated intellectual women. Nora expressed to Samuel Beckett her exasperation with those who praised Joyce's deep understanding of a woman's viewpoint, 'That man knows nothing about women' (quoted in Maddox, op cit p. 278). Joyce talked of the 'Penelope' episode as a coda, saying that the book proper ended with 'Ithaca'. He also, however, told Frank Budgen that Molly was the axis upon which the whole book revolved.

One of the prime themes of *Ulysses* is the importance of paternity and some feminist critics have seen women, and particularly Molly, as marginalized by this emphasis. Molly is clearly linked to the flow of life: the tumbling words of her uninhibited monologue coming like water over the dry rocks of the scientific precision of Ithaca and the rambling aridity of Eumaeus. Molly is the life principle and male critics have associated her with the womb, with Nature, with the earth Mother and with an animal goddess.

Molly

Some feminist critics have resented this association of woman with the purely physical, playing no part in the worlds of ideas and art. Susan Gilbert and Sandra Gubar see Joyce as confining woman, giving her no existence outside her body. Feminist critics who share this viewpoint indicate, tellingly, that Molly is never seen out of bed, save as a disembodied arm at a window and that her first word in the novel is not even a proper word: 'Mn', rather like the cat's 'mrkgnao'. Her ignorance and attitude are established early on when, having asked Bloom the meaning of the word 'metempsychosis', which she pronounces 'met-him-pike-hoses', she dismisses her husband's attempts to explain. Her preferred reading matter is *Ruby: The Pride of the Ring*, although she complains 'There's nothing smutty in it.' Molly is seen by some feminist critics as a caricature typifying a male view of woman. Her spectacularly successful copulation with Boylan is just a male masturbatory fantasy, and Molly, the 'fat heap ... with a back on her like a ballalley' as the narrator of Cyclops describes her, is just a cartoon, a man's view of woman.

Other feminist critics have taken a different view of Molly, however, and much feminist writing interprets Joyce as other than a writer at the head of a patriarchal literary heritage. This view of Molly sees her as an anarchic figure, mocking and overturning all the male certitudes and values which have been expressed in the rest of the book. What men find deadly serious, she finds ridiculous. Where the men in the book are detached from their emotions, regarding them at a distance, Molly is gloriously in touch with hers. She is not fooled by Boylan. The view of the suspicious narrator of the 'Cyclops' episode may echo male triumphalism: 'That's the bucko that'll organise her, take my tip', but the reality is different. Molly's monologue shows that it is *Molly* who is using Boylan for the sexual gratification she is denied at home. She does not find him satisfying in any other way, however, and remarks upon his limitations and his gross familiarity, resenting the slap on the behind he gave her. Her affirmation at the end of the book is for Bloom – although, as always, it is tempered by practicality: 'I saw he understood or felt what a woman is and I knew I could always get round him.' As Brenda Maddox points out from seeing Molly as a woman who subverts male authority, it is but a short step to 'Molly-worship', although other critics are more sceptical.

THE WOMEN IN DUBLINERS
The women in *Dubliners* are, like the men, trapped by the general paralysis of the city and its life, but they are even worse off: they are 'the oppressed of the oppressed', as Karen Lawrence says. The women are

often defined in terms of men, such as Corley's woman in 'Two Gallants', or Evelina who wants Frank to take her away, but who, in the end, cannot go, or Mrs Sinico in 'A Painful Case', whose temerity in speaking of her feelings to Mr Duffy leads to her rejection and, ultimately, her death. Deeply frustrated men like Farrington in 'Counterparts' will relieve their frustrations upon deeply frustrated wives and families. Those women who, one way or another, have managed to forge their own way, do so either by playing the masculine game or, like Maria in 'Clay', by simply accepting the limits of their lives. 'The Dead', however, is a much richer field for exploration.

Women in 'The Dead'

As 'The Dead' shifts attention to the middle-class cultural life of Dublin, we might expect to see women playing a different role and, indeed, the evening at the Morkans sees Gabriel Conroy confronted by women who, in various ways, challenge him and lead him to the epiphany he undergoes at the end. The conventional view of the story is that Conroy, a decent, cultured, liberal man, is shown that his image of himself falls short of reality and that the life he leads is shallow and complacent. The story, and the collection, ends on a note of optimism as Conroy looks westward to the real Ireland and the epiphanic possibility of 'the full glory of some passion'. The vehicles for Conroy's epiphany are three women: Miss Ivors, an intellectual who upbraids him for neglecting his own native culture; his wife, whose story of the young man who died for love of her shows Gabriel how far he falls short of his ideal; and the maid, Lily, whose opening remark to him, 'the men that is now is only all palaver and what they can get out of you', makes him blush, and prefigures the revelation at the end of the story. Surely here we have the genuine voice of women exposing the complacency beneath an apparently smooth surface.

Margot Norris

Feminist critics are not so sanguine. Margot Norris looks further than the effect of the women on Gabriel Conroy and deals with their portrayal. She sees the story as consisting of a:

Loud and audible male narration challenged and disrupted by a silent or discounted female countertext that does not, in the end, succeed in making itself heard.

'Not the Girl She Was At All: Women in The Dead' in Schwarz, D.R., (1994), p. 192

Norris suggests that the reader is invited, throughout, to agree with Gabriel's view, as he argues with the critical Molly Ivors or admires his wife as she stands on the stairs. The women's voices are not the genuine expression of women's views but artifices designed to help us see as Gabriel sees. This view would seem to place Margaret Norris on the side of those who regard Joyce's portrayal of women with disfavour. From this point, however, her thinking takes an interesting turn. She writes that, although the narration favours the patriarchal, there are 'gaps and contradictions' which, whether Joyce intended them or not, introduce notes of scepticism which encourage questions. She cites Julia Morkan's distress at the recent papal decree that female singers should be banned from church choirs, the narrator commenting upon the extraordinary beauty and strength of her voice, seeming explicitly to underline the unfairness and narrowness of the decree. 'The Dead', she concludes, is predominantly patriarchal, but leaves loopholes through which alternative interpretations are possible.

Suzette Henke

Suzette Henke, in her essay 'Stephen Dedalus and Women', shows us the extent to which, in *Portrait*, women are treated as extensions of Stephen's inner state rather than as characters in their own right. We do, of course, see everything in the book from Stephen's eyes and those eyes are extraordinarily self-regarding. Stephen's ideas of women exist within a framework of opposites, primarily in a dichotomy between spirit and flesh in which women are associated with the physical – a charge levelled often by feminist critics of Joyce.

Henke writes that Stephen's image of women tends to the stereotypes of virgin and whore. We watch Stephen becoming masculinised by the culture around him, his education, his family and so on. The Christmas argument over Parnell, for example, establishes women as either the champions of the repressive Church or pacifiers, while the two men seem to be arguing for something freer and more noble. The sight of the men moved to tears affects Stephen and the story of Mr Casey spitting in the eye of the woman protester stays with him. His reading of 'The Count of Monte Cristo' leads to his association of himself with the hero and romantic fantasies about the heroine, Mercedes.

In the same way, having met Emma Clery, he reconstructs her from his own fantasies and predilections. Henke makes this clear with her account of the scene in which Emma walks with Stephen to the tram stop and Stephen does not take advantage of what he sees as her wish for him to kiss her. Describing this as a 'self-indulgent exercise', Henke writes:

> On the verge of losing composure, Stephen refuses to yield to that purported temptress. Like the Count of Monte Cristo, he turns away from Emma in proud abnegation, determined to possess his mistress through art.

Kershner, R.B. (ed.), (1993), p. 313

Stephen's poetry is an unconscious attempt to distance himself from real relationships and real involvement with real women: all is personalised, symbolised, idealised, sanctified. The sight of the girl on the beach which provides him with his final epiphany is, after all, yet another projection of stereotypes: a 'profane virgin', a woman 'mortal and angelic, sensuous and sane'.

In the encounter with the prostitute with whom Stephen finds a sort of release, Henke sees a reversal in which it is Stephen who becomes the one who yields. She shows how, despite the dark, obsessive language in which the pursuit of a prostitute is described, during the actual encounter, it is Stephen who is passive:

> His lips would not bend to kiss her. He wanted to be held firmly in her arms, to be caressed slowly, slowly, slowly. In her arms, he felt that he had suddenly become strong and fearless and sure of himself. But his lips would not bend to kiss her.

In the mixture of eroticism and romanticism, in the beautiful prose of this passage, Stephen resembles 'both a sacrificial victim and a child about to burst into hysterical weeping', the prostitute having overtones both of mother and priestess.

Like Norris, Henke gives Joyce the benefit of the doubt. She sees the irony in Joyce's presentation of Stephen and concludes that Joyce 'seems to imply that the developing artist's notorious misogyny will prove to be still another dimension (and limitation) of his youthful priggishness'.

One of the most interesting aspects of feminist criticism is the question of how far a male author such as Joyce is displaying his own chauvinism, and how far he is revealing the chauvinistic assumptions that have shaped the world about which he writes.

JOYCE AND PSYCHOANALYTICAL CRITICISM

Psychoanalytical criticism has its beginnings in the work of Sigmund Freud, whose theories have had such a far ranging influence on the way in which we think of and try to understand ourselves. Freud constructed a model of human behaviour and motive stressing the complex structure of the mind. The conscious mind is the rational part of our minds with which we conduct day-to-day business and with which we form our images of ourselves. The unconscious mind is the repository for all the experiences, sense memories, traumas, forbidden desires and so on which are suppressed and hidden from us. It was Freud's contention that the sources of human motivation were primarily unconscious rather than conscious. The secret world of our unconscious sometimes emerges in actions which appear involuntary, such as dreams, sudden uncharacteristic behaviour or in slips of the tongue, known as Freudian slips, which reveal the actual desire or fear which the conscious mind tries to repress.

> **KEY TERM**
>
> Psychoanalytical criticism criticism which applies the theories of Sigmund Freud to textual analysis and in particular looks at the unconscious motivations of both authors and characters.

Freudian slips

A classic example of such a slip occurs in *Ulysses*, as Bloom stands in Barney Keirnan's with The Citizen and others. All day, Bloom's conscious mind has been turning away from the afternoon tryst between his wife and Boylan but it is there in his unconscious, repressed, stifled and revealed when, discussing how Mrs Dignam might benefit from an insurance deal, he says: 'Well that's a point ... for the wife's admirers. Whose admirers? says Joe. The wife's advisers, I mean, says Bloom. Then he starts all confused and mucking it up ...'

Dreams as coded messages

For Freud, these repressions are, in part, a result of our socialisation as children, when we learn, or are taught, what is acceptable and what is not, what is rewarded and what punished, what pleasures will be encouraged and what pleasures must not be indulged. Infantile sexuality, feelings about parents are repressed. Dreams may be disguised expressions of these repressed impulses, dredged up in a coded form while the censor of the conscious mind is unwary. These codes are symbols which represent the true meaning of what has been dreamt about. In analysis, dreams may be decoded, and neuroses – the mental disorders resulting from a clash between conscious and unconscious – may be cured. Interpreting symbols is at the centre of Freudian thought.

Joyce denied Freudian influence

Early Freudian critics treated works of literature as vehicles through which the authors could be psychoanalysed, while others applied psychoanalytical technique to the study of characters. A later school looked at the relationship between author, text and reader and the ways in which authors address the reader's unconscious. Joyce professed a distaste for Freud and strongly denied that he had made use of Freudian tenets in *Ulysses*. The inspiration for his use of stream of consciousness he credited to a book by Edouard Dujardin, *Les Lauriers sont coupés*, a soliloquy without any intervention from an authorial voice. Similarly, although the 'Circe' episode, with its catalogue of repressed desires, guilty secrets and furtive acts dragged into the light and personified seems quintessentially Freudian, Joyce gave no credit at all to Freudian theories, although he had, from an early age, maintained an interest in dreams and interpretations of them.

ANALYSIS OF PORTRAIT

A psychoanalytical critique such as Sheldon Brivic's account of *Portrait of the Artist as a Young Man* begins by assuming that, although some of the constructions, images and patterns in the novel will have been consciously derived, some will have come from the author's own unconscious. The novel is about a young man whose development as an artist depends upon his shedding the influences which surround him: family, church, society and country. Although these separations are justified in rational terms, the psychoanalytical critic goes deeper and looks at the factors which sow the seeds of this alienation in Stephen's unconscious. Thus decisions and actions which seem to have been made deliberately and rationally have their origins in the unconscious and it is the job of the critic to reveal reality by analysing not only the actions and behaviour of the character, but also the language used by the author to describe them.

Thus, Brivic looks carefully at the first six years of Stephen's life. He notes the contrasts in Stephen's memories of his parents, 'his mother had a nicer smell than his father', and equates the memory of the threat of eagles pulling out his eyes if he did not apologise with the fear of castration which Freud says is the consequence of the Oedipal stage of development in which the male child longs for genital contact with his mother. When Stephen leaves for Conglowes, his mother kisses him goodbye, telling him not to mix with the 'rough boys'. She lifts up her veil 'and her nose and her eyes were red'. Brivic notes the underlying sexuality in the images of what he calls 'moist, pink exposure', and sees the following dream of home as picking up and expanding the earlier difference between the warmth and comfort of maternity and the cold harshness of the father.

So the development of the artist is shaped by these workings below conscious level and rationalised by the conscious mind. Stephen's facility for and fascination with language is a way of controlling reality, in a way, a substitute for reality. The beginnings of Stephen's artistic and intellectual development lie in the defences he builds up against conflict. His need to become an artist is a blind, a 'myth generated by his neurotic need to alienate himself again and again from that which he feels he cannot have' (Sheldon Brivic, 'The Disjunctive Structure of Joyce's Portrait' in Kershner, op cit p. 261).

Psychoanalytical criticism applies the tenets of psychoanalytical theory to present radically different pictures from those arrived at by conventional critical methods, not only revealing underlying impulses and motivations implicit in the text, but reinterpreting what is presented as explicit. This form of criticism also offers analysis, not just of the book as a text, but also what it can reveal of the author's unconscious structures.

Joyce is fascinating to psychoanalytical critics partly because, as was said earlier, his work seems to contain in itself possible interpretations of it and to engage with it. Joyce seems to have anticipated and engaged with the varieties of interpretations which have been applied to his books. He stated the intention to ensure his immortality through enigmas and puzzles which would keep discussion raging and, as it is hoped this book has shown, he has succeeded.

✳ ✳ ✳ ✳ SUMMARY ✳ ✳ ✳ ✳

- Joyce is a modernist because he seems to have anticipated and addressed interpretations of his work in his books.

- Modern critical schools discuss Joyce from different perspectives.

- Feminist critics seem either to mistrust him, his presentation of and attitude towards women, or see his accurate presentation of the patriarchal attitudes of his characters as allowing for feminist interpretations.

- Psychoanalytical critics examine his characters, his hidden motivations in the presentation of his characters and his relationship with the reader.

Where Next?

9

Depending upon what has caught your interest most, there are many directions in which you could turn from here.

THE BOOKS

Ulysses

You may choose to go back to the beginning of *Ulysses* for a second reading: you will see so much more than you did at the first reading. If you do, it would be a good idea to do it in the company of two men:

Stuart Gilbert, *James Joyce's Ulysses* (1952). This book will give you great insight into the book's structure and scheme and help you understand the various correspondences and symbols.

Harry Blamires, *The Bloomsday Book* (1966). This is a page-by-page guide to *Ulysses* and delightful to read alongside the book. The effect is like strolling through a city in the company of a knowledgeable, enthusiastic and extremely entertaining guide.

Another interesting, but rather sceptical and dissenting, view can be found in Robert Martin Adams' *Surface and Symbol: The Consistency of James Joyce's Ulysses* (1962).

Other works

You may wish to read those of Joyce's works which fell outside the main scope of this introduction. There are two volumes of poems, *Chamber Music* (1907) and *Pomes Penyeach* (1927) which, along with the play *Exiles* (1918) and some uncollected poems can be found bound together in a single Penguin paperback. You may feel brave enough to tackle *Finnegans Wake*, in which case, there are several good guides on the market, and an excellent introduction by Anthony Burgess called *Here Comes Everybody* (1965).

BIOGRAPHY

If you would like to pursue the life story, then Richard Ellman's biography *James Joyce* is still the definitive version. It is interesting, however, to supplement Ellman and see from different angles. Two books which are immensely readable and engrossing are Brenda Maddox's biography of Nora Barnacle called simply *Nora* (1988) and Edna O'Brien's *James Joyce* (1999). This is a short book with no footnotes which is written with all the style and wit which you would expect from Edna O'Brien: it is a more impressionistic portrait, the perfect foil for Ellman.

A close examination of Joyce's early years may be found in Peter Costello's *James Joyce: The Years of Growth, 1882–1915* (1992).

It is also a good idea to find Frank Budgen's *James Joyce and the Making of Ulysses* (1972), referred to in the text. The accounts of conversations with Joyce on many topics are interesting, as is an account of Zurich during and shortly after the First World War, and his observations on both *Ulysses* and *Finnegans Wake.*

If you want to hear more of Joyce's own voice, the *Selected Letters*, edited by Richard Ellman, are available in paperback from Faber.

CRITICISM

Contemporary and traditional

Highly recommended is the two-volume collection *James Joyce: the Critical Heritage* edited by Robert H. Deming (1970). These are early reviews, reactions and critical essays gathered together. They span the years 1907 to 1941 which are fascinating. They show the extent to which what Joyce did was revolutionary. They show the initial shock and incomprehension, the attempts to make sense of what was being read and the gradual realisation that these books were works of genius.

Modern critical approaches

The field is wide indeed when it comes to modern criticism. Any list is bound to be very selective, but the following are informative and, just as important, comprehensible.

'The Dead' and *Portrait of the Artist as a Young Man* are both published in the series *Case Studies in Modern Criticism*, and each is followed by an excellent selection of essays from the points of view of psychoanalytical, feminist, reader-response, deconstructionalist and new historicist criticism. Once you have read these, you may be clearer about the direction in which you wish to move. Some further recommendations are:

Richard Brown, *James Joyce and Sexuality* (1985) and *James Joyce: A Post Culturalist Perspective* (1992).

Daniel R. Schwarz, *Reading Joyce's Ulysses* (1987).

James Fairhall, *James Joyce and the Question of History* (1993).

There is also an excellent compendium of modern criticism edited by Derek Attridge, *The Cambridge Companion to James Joyce* (1990).

SOURCES AND BACKGROUNDS

If you are interested in the wealth of ideas, myth, wide reading, philosophy, theology, geography and the minutiae of personal experience upon which the books were founded, then there are two seemingly exhaustive, but still developing, studies by Don Gifford: *Joyce Annotated* (1982) and *Ulysses Annotated* (1988). These are both available in paperback and operate as massive footnotes to all three of the books dealt with in this introduction. They are immensely browseable.

Worth finding is Frank Delaney's *James Joyce's Odyssey: A Guide to the Dublin of Ulysses* (1981), which is a pictorial tour in the footsteps of Mr Bloom.

A fascinating study of the battles of various sorts surrounding the publication of *Ulysses* is to be found in Bruce Arnold's *The Scandal of Ulysses* (1991).

OTHER MEDIA

There are various versions of *Portrait* available on audiobooks and a first-rate reading of *Dubliners* by T.P. McKenna which is available now in a 'special limited edition'.

John Huston's last film, a moving adaptation of 'The Dead' (1987), is well worth seeing.

Joseph Strick very bravely filmed both *Portrait* (1979) and *Ulysses* (1967). It was this last film which accounted for a brief public interest in Joyce in the late 1960s when Lady Dartmouth, having seen it, pronounced it obscene and disgraceful.

In both films, Maurice Roeves plays Stephen Dedalus. One of the delights of the film of *Portrait* is that the late Sir John Gielgud delivers the pivotal sermon of Father Arnall. The film of *Ulysses*, is, presumably for financial reasons, set in modern, 1960s', Dublin. It is a remarkable attempt to film what seems to be unfilmable and really does have its moments. Milo O'Shea is such a skilful actor and his performance so persuasive that one forgets he does not resemble Bloom at all; T.P. McKenna is a wonderful Buck Mulligan and Barbara Jefford a superb Molly. Her reading of the final monologue is also a reason to hunt down a soundtrack album, two vinyl LPS, released by Caedmon records.

Also of great interest is the film based on Brenda Maddox's book, *Nora*, directed by Pat Murphy, with Ewan McGregor as Joyce and Susan Lynch as Nora.

These recommendations are simply scratching the surface and most will yield bibliographies of their own which, again, you may wish to pursue.

✳ ✳ ✳ ✳*SUMMARY* ✳ ✳ ✳ ✳

- Read Joyce's books and other work.

- Read the standard commentaries.

- Read his biography.

- Tackle the academic criticism.

Joyce the exile.

GLOSSARY

Allusion Indirect reference. Joyce's books are full of echoes of his own life, other works of literature, myths, biblical stories and so on. Much research has been done on allusions in Joyce.

Bathos The use of anti-climax for comic effect: building up to a climax which is then undermined by being less than expected.

Epic A long narrative poem written in lofty style which deals with matters of great importance, celebrating a great theme and glorifying a great hero. A **comic epic** applies epic principles to lesser matter.

Epiphany The word Joyce uses to describe a moment in which an experience reveals its inner meaning.

Feminist criticism Looks at the presentation of women, ways in which masculine ideology is carried in texts and the undervaluing of woman writers. More recently the term has become broader, studying all texts from a female perspective and looking at the relationships between men and women in the light of the gender debate.

Hemiplegia A medical term employed by Joyce to represent what he saw as the paralysis affecting Dublin and its citizens.

Hero In the classical sense, a man of superhuman powers, a demigod.

Irony A figure of speech in which the implied meaning is the opposite of what has actually been said or written.

New Historicism Criticism which seeks to see works of literature in their historical and cultural contexts.

Parody An exaggerated imitation of another piece of writing, usually for comic effect. Parodies abound in the Cyclops episode of *Ulysses*.

Psychoanalytical criticism Criticism which applies the theories of Sigmund Freud to textual analysis and in particular looks at the unconscious motivations of both authors and characters.

Stream of consciousness Writing which attempts to reproduce exactly and in real time the apparently random sequences of thought which stream through our minds.

Structuralism The idea that all elements of human culture can be understood as a system of signs.

Symbol A sign which represents something else. In *Ulysses*, Nelson's Pillar, then standing in Dublin, might be seen as a symbol of colonial triumphalism and oppression.

CHRONOLOGY OF MAJOR WORKS

1900 Article on Ibsen published
1906 Completes *Dubliners*
Begins to shape *Portrait of the Artist as a Young Man*
1907 *Music*, volume of poetry, published
1914 *Dubliners* published
Portrait begins serialisation in *The Egoist*
Starts work on *Ulysses*
1916 Publication of *Portrait* in America
1919 Play *Exiles* published
Ulysses begins serialisation in *The Little Review*
1921 Serialisation of *Ulysses* halted on grounds of obscenity
1922 *Ulysses* published in Paris
1923 Begins work on *Finnegans Wake*
1927 *Pomes Penyeach* published
1934 *Ulysses* published in book form in America
1936 *Ulysses* published in Britain
1939 *Finnegans Wake* published

FURTHER READING

Arnold, B. *The Scandal of Ulysses*, Sinclair Stevenson (1991)

Adams, R.M. *Surface and Symbol*, Oxford University Press (1962)

Attridge, D. (ed.) *Cambridge Companion to James Joyce*, Cambridge University Press (1990)

Blades, J., *James Joyce: Portrait of the Artist as a Young Man*, Penguin (1991)

Blamires, H., *The Bloomsday Book*, Methuen & Co. (1966)

Blamires, H., *Studying James Joyce*, Longman (1986)

Bolt, S., *A Preface to James Joyce*, Longman (1981)

Brown, R., *James Joyce and Sexuality*, Cambridge University Press (1985)

Brown, R., *James Joyce: A Post-Culturalist Perspective*, Macmillan (1992)

Budgen, F., *James Joyce and the Making of Ulysses*, Oxford University Press (1972)

Burgess, A. *Here Comes Everybody*, Faber (1965)

Costello, P., *James Joyce: The Years of Growth 1882–1915*, Kyle Cathie (1992)

Delaney, F., *James Joyce's Odyssey*, Hodder & Stoughton (1981)

Deming, R.H., *James Joyce: The Critical Heritage, Vols 1 and 2*, Routledge & Kegan Paul (1970)

Eagleton, T., *Literary Theory: An Introduction*, Basil Blackwell (1983)

Ellman, R., *James Joyce*, Oxford University Press (1959)

Fairhall, J., *James Joyce and the Question of History*, Cambridge University Press (1993)

Gifford, D., *Joyce Annotated*, University of California Press (1982)

Gifford, D., *Ulysses Annotated*, University of California Press (1988)

Gilbert, S., *James Joyce's Ulysses – A Study*, Penguin (1930, rev. 1952)

Gilbert, S. and Gubar, S., 'Sexual linguistics, gender, language and sexuality', New Literary History 16 (1985)

Joyce, J., *Portrait of the Artist as a Young Man*, Ellman, R. (ed.) Jonathan Cape (1964)

Joyce, J., *Dubliners*, Scholes, R. (ed.) Jonathan Cape (1971)

Joyce, J., *Selected Letters of James Joyce*, Faber (1975)

Joyce, J., *Ulysses*, Gabler, HW. (ed.) Penguin (1984)

Joyce, J., *Poems and Exiles*, Mayes, J.C.C. (ed.) Penguin (1992)

Joyce, S., *My Brother's Keeper*, Viking (1958)

Kershner, R.B. (ed.), *Portrait of the Artist as a Young Man: Case Studies in Contemporary Criticism*, Bedford Books of St. Martin's Press (1993)

Leavis, F.R., *The Great Tradition*, Chatto & Windus (1948)

Levin, H., *James Joyce: A Critical Introduction*, Faber (1941)

Maddox, B., *Nora*, Hamish Hamilton (1988)

O'Brien, E., *James Joyce*, Weidenfeld & Nicolson (1999)

Schwarz, D.R., *Reading Joyce's Ulysses*, Macmillan (1987)

Schwarz, D.R., *The Dead: Case Studies in Contemporary Criticism*, Bedford Books of St. Martin's Press (1994)

Sherry, V., *Joyce – Ulysses*, Cambridge University Press (1994)

Tindall, W.Y., *James Joyce: His Ways of Interpreting the Modern World*, New York, Scribner (1950)

Tindall, W.Y., *A Readers Guide*, NY, Farrar, Strand and Giroux (1959)

INDEX

Adams, Robert Martin 74
Allusion 13
Animal Farm 45
Arnold, Bruce 76
Attidge, Derek 76
Auden, W.H. 5
Austen, Jane 19, 58

Bathos 30
Beach, Sylvia 9, 31
Belvedere College 6
Blamires, Harry 74
Bloom, Leopold 8, 12, 21, 32–48, 62
Bloom, Molly 8, 12, 32–48, 64, 65
Bloomsday 8, 32
Brivic, Sheldon 71–72
Budgen, Frank 31, 53, 55–56, 64, 75
Burgess, Anthony 1, 74

Cape, Jonathan 15
'Chamber Music' 50, 74
Chekhov, Anton 50
Clongowes College 5, 26, 72
Colum, Mary 64
Comic epic 35
Costello, Peter 57, 58
Conrad, Joseph 57, 58

'Count of Monte Cristo' 27, 68
Crane, Hart 52

Daily Express 54
caedalus and Icarus 25, 36
de Maupassant, Guy 50
Dedalus, Stephen 3, 12, 21, 24–30, 33, 35–44, 52, 62, 64, 72, 77
Delaney, Frank 76
Deming, Robert H 53, 54, 75
Dickens, Charles
Dublin 3, 5, 7, 8, 9, 11, 12, 14–22, 32
Dubliners 1, 2, 3, 8, 9, 11, 14–22, 23–24, 29, 31, 44, 50, 51 65–67
Duckworths 50, 51
Dujardin, Edouard 71

Eagleton, Terry 59
'Egoist' 1, 9, 23, 51
Eliot, George 58
Eliot, T.S. 1, 55, 58
Ellman, Richard 5, 8, 32, 55, 57, 59–60, 75

epic 55
epiphany 18, 19, 21, 37, 66
'Exiles' 74

Fairhall, James 76
feminist criticism 62, 63–69
Fielding, Henry 19, 63
Finnegan's Wake 1, 10, 49, 57, 74, 75
Flaubert, Gustave 50, 52, 55
Forster, E.M. 51
'Fortnightly Review' 7
Freud, Sigmund 69–71
Frye, Northrop 62

Gabler, Hans Walter 32
Garnett, Edward 57
Gielgud, Sir John 77
Gifford, Don 76
Gilbert, Stuart 55–57, 64, 74
Gogarthy, Oliver St John 8, 49
Gorky, Maxim 50
Gould, Gerald 50
'Guardian' 52
Gubar, Sandra 64

Hackett, Francis 51
Hamlet 38, 40

Hazlitt, William 61
hemiplegia 15
Henke, Suzette 67–68
hero 35
Homer's Odyssey 33–34, 38–43
Hopkins, G.M. 58
Huston, John 77

Ibsen, Henrik 7, 50
Irish Homestead 14, 24, 50
irony 20, 30

James, Henry 58
Jefford, Barbara 77
Johnson, Dr. Samuel 61
Joyce, Giorgio 8, 9
Joyce, James (passim)
Joyce, John 5–7, 10
Joyce, Lucia 8, 10
Joyce, Mary 5–7
Joyce, Nora (Barnacle) 8, 10, 49, 56, 75
Joyce, Stanislaus 5, 8, 24, 49
Jung, C.G. 10

Larbaud, Valery 55
Lawrence, D.H. 51, 55, 58
Lawrence, Karen 61
Leavis, F.R. 57, 61, 63
Leslie, Shane 53
Levin, Harry 59
Little Review 9, 31, 52

Lynch, Susan 77

Maddox, Brenda 32, 39, 64, 65, 75, 77
McGregor, Ewan 77
McKenna, T.P. 77
Moore, George 50
Murphy, Pat 77

New Historicism 63
New Republic 51
New Statesman 50
Norris, Margot 66, 69
Nouvelle Revue 55

O'Brien, Edna 75
O'Shea, Milo 77

Paris 7, 9, 32, 36
Parnell, Charles Stuart 6, 20, 26, 52, 63, 68
Parody 35
Pilgrim's Progress 45
Pomes Penyeach 10, 74
Portrait of the Artist 1–3, 5–9, 11–12, 17, 23–30, 35–36, 44, 50–52, 55, 59, 67–79, 71–72, 77
Pound, Ezra 19, 31, 51, 52, 55
psychoanalytical criticism 62, 69–73

Quinn, John 52

Richards, Grant 14, 16
Richards, I.R. 58–59, 61

Roeves, Maurice 77

Schwarz, Daniel R. 76
Shakespeare, William 4, 8, 40
Stephen Hero 7, 23, 59
Strick, Joseph 77
structuralism 61, 62

Tindall, William York 59
Trieste 8, 32
Trollope, Anthony 44

Ulysses 1–3, 8–11, 21, 30–48, 52–53, 57, 59, 62, 65, 70–71, 74, 75, 77
Updike, John 1
University College 7

Weaver, Harriet Shaw 1, 9, 31, 51
Wells, H.G. 52
Wilson, Edmund 59
Woolf, Viginia 1, 52, 55

Yeats, W.B. 1, 50, 52

Zola, Emile 50
Zurich 8, 9, 32, 56

VIRGINIA WOOLF – A BEGINNER'S GUIDE

Gina Wisker

Virginia Woolf – A Beginner's Guide introduces you to the life and works of Virginia Woolf. It reveals her as emotionally insightful, exploring the texture of changing relationships, expressing from the inside how it feels to be alive. Discover how Woolf challenges the conventions of the novel, recreating and representing life rather than becoming enslaved by plot.

Gina Wisker's text explores:

- how to approach the great works
- Woolf's ideas about gender, writing and power
- Woolf as an experimental writer and the influence she has had on many writers since
- the way these ideas have provided us with insights into the lives of both men and women.

The facts … the concepts … the ideas …

MARCEL PROUST – A BEGINNER'S GUIDE

Ingrid Wassennar

Marcel Proust – A Beginner's Guide introduces you to the life and works of Proust. He is shown as a writer who has influenced not only the way we approach literature but also the way we think about ourselves. Discover how *A La Recherche du Temps Perdu* is relevant to today's technology-intensive and individualistic society.

Ingrid Wassenaar's text explores:

- how to approach *A La Recherche du Temps Perdu* (*In Search of Lost Time*)
- Proust's ideas on topics such as time, memory and sexuality
- modern critical approches to Proust and his ideas
- the relevance of these ideas to readers in the twenty-first century.

The facts … the concepts … the ideas …

CHARLES DICKENS – A BEGINNER'S GUIDE

Rob Abbott and Charlie Bell

Charles Dickens – A Beginner's Guide introduces you to the life and works of Charles Dickens. The book shows him to have been a writer who is both enjoyable and accessible to the modern reader. A great Victorian and prolific novelist Dickens has a profound influence on the way his contemporaries saw their society and the way we today view the Victorians. In exploring four of the most popular novels *Bleak House*, *Oliver Twist*, *Hard Times* and *Great Expectations* the writers show the relevance of Dickens today and help readers to develop their own responses to the works.

Rob Abbott and Charlie Bell's informative text explores:

- how to approach the novels and short stories
- Dickens' ideas on subjects such as morality, poverty and the place of women
- contemporary critical approaches to Dickens and his work
- the influence of Dickens both in his own lifetime and in the twenty-first century.

The facts … the concepts … the ideas …